MU

MULL
& IONA

P. A. Macnab

David and Charles

ACKOWLEDGEMENTS

To the memory of a patient and loving
wife who shared my enthusiasms and love
of Mull; and to my many friends on the
island with whom I 'tired the sun with
talking, and sent him down in the sky'.

A DAVID & CHARLES BOOK

Copyright © David & Charles Limited
1995

David & Charles is an imprint
of F&W Media International, Ltd
Brunel House, Forde Close,
Newton Abbot, TQ12 4PU, UK

F&W Media International, Ltd
is a subsidiary of F+W Media, Inc
10151 Carver Road, Suite #200,
Blue Ash, OH 45242, USA

First published in the UK in 1995
Reprinted 1997, 2001, 2003, 2005,
2006, 2009, 2011, 2012, 2013, 2015

Text Copyright © P. A. Macnab
1995–2008
Photography © Derek Croucher
1995–2008

Map on p. 6 by Ethan Danielson

P. A. Macnab has asserted his right to
be identified as author of this work in
accordance with the Copyright, Designs
and Patents Act, 1988.

A catalogue record for this book is
available from the British Library.

ISBN-13: 978-0-7153-2892-7 paperback
ISBN-10: 0-7153-2892-1 paperback

Printed in China by WKT Co Ltd for
David & Charles
Brunel House   Newton Abbot   Devon

David & Charles publish high quality
books on a wide range of subjects.
For more great book ideas visit:
www.fwmedia.co.uk

CONTENTS

Left: The north coast of Iona

*Half title: (Clockwise from top left) Pony trekking beside Loch Ba;
Calgary Bay looking south - one of the cleanest, clearest and most
attractive bays on the whole west coast of Britain; Ulva - columnar
basalts in the cliff overlooking Loch na Keal, Ben More and the
central mountains in the foreground and (right) the forbidding
cliffs of Gribun; the vast entrance of MacKinnon's Cave (see p79)
(Photos: Author)*

Title page: Across Loch Scridain from Killiemore

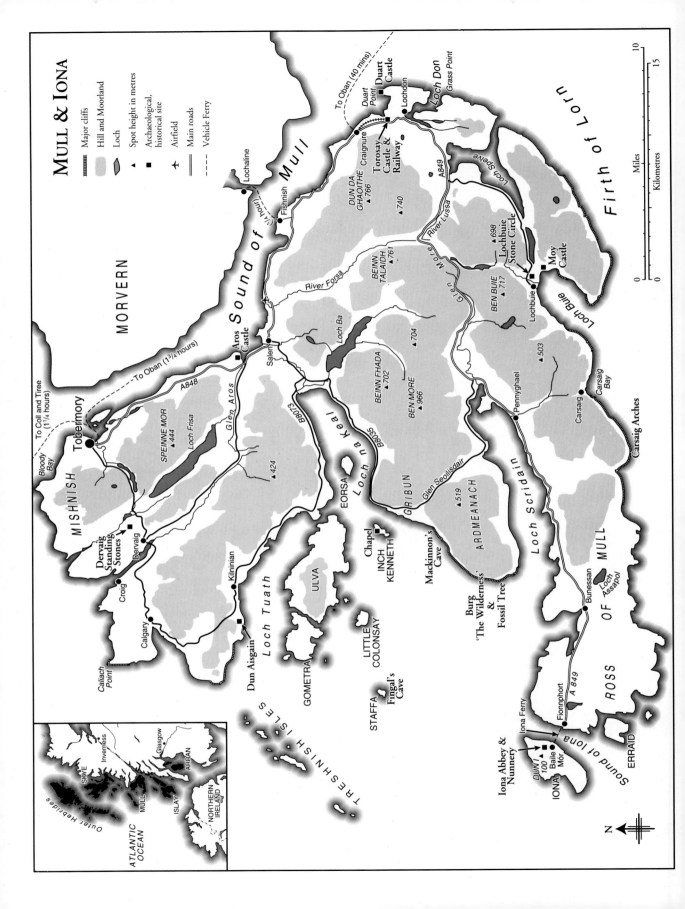

INTRODUCTION

MULL, THE ANCIENT MALIOS of Ptolemy, is the third largest of the Hebridean Islands; it is 225,000 acres (90,000ha) in extent, and is roughly 24 miles (38km) from north to south and 26 miles (42km) from east to west. Broken up by deeply penetrating sea-lochs and inlets, these figures give no indication of the length of its coastline – 300 miles (480km) – nor of its road system, which has about 140 miles (225km) of roads varying from good to passable. It is separated from the Scottish mainland by the Sound of Mull to the north-east, which turns south-west into the Firth of Lorne.

Oban is the main approach from the mainland. It is the rail terminus from Glasgow and the south and has been described as the 'Charing Cross of the Highlands'. There are direct sailings to nearly all the southern Hebridean islands by ships of the Caledonian-MacBrayne fleet, the life-line of the Hebrides for nearly 150 years and without which many small communities would practically cease to exist.

THE COMING OF CHRISTIANITY

The sacred island of Iona, together with at least fourteen pre-Reformation chapels – now ruinous – scattered throughout Mull, remind us that here was the real cradle of Christianity in Scotland, extending to Scandinavia and the Rhine Valley, following the arrival in Iona in 563 of St Columba and his missionary companions.

Above: Evening light over Loch Beg

The steadily increasing popularity of Mull and Iona is well brought out in the comparative figures between 1967 and 1993 for the number of passengers and vehicles conveyed between Mull and the mainland:

Route	Passengers	Vehicles
Oban – Craignure	516,194	84,904
Fishnish – Lochaline	97,835	37,888
Tobermory – Kilchoan	22,000	3,668
Fionnphort – Iona	248,687	No cars
Total for 1993	**884,716**	**126,460**
Total for 1967	**199,000**	**17,496**

The crossing from Oban to Craignure, the ferry terminus in Mull, takes only forty minutes and there are several journeys daily at the height of the season by the one hundred car ferry. Starting from the Glasgow area, the popular route to Oban – about 100 miles (160km) distant – is by Loch Lomond and Crianlarich, where road and rail branch off towards Fort William and Mallaig, and to the right for the east of Scotland. However, while the Loch Lomond road is indeed romantic and picturesque, it is a busy one, with some stretches still to be upgraded. Better that the traveller heads for Greenock and Gourock by the M8 motorway passing Glasgow Airport, and joins the half-hourly Cal-Mac ferry across the Firth of Clyde to Dunoon; this takes about 15–20 minutes.

Alternatively, at the urban west end of Gourock, Western Ferries runs a similar but shorter ferry to Hunters' Quay, on the Holy Loch. Clear of the village there is a highly picturesque stretch of road which runs beside narrow, six-mile long Loch Eck with its mountainous beauty, to Loch Fyne and Inveraray, joining the Oban road at Dalmally; this is a fine, quiet, fast road, and it is eighty miles from Dunoon to Oban.

Travelling south to Mull from Inverness and Loch Ness, there are two routes to Mull, either by Oban, or by the quieter Corran Ferry (five minutes) over Loch Linnhe and across Morvern to Lochaline on the Sound of Mull, where a twelve-car ferry shuttles over to Fishnish in Mull. There is a third but more isolated approach from Kilchoan in Ardnamurchan, the most westerly point of mainland Britain, to Tobermory. This twice-daily crossing, once for passengers only, now transports cars without booking, like Fishnish.

> An t-Eilean Muileach, an t-eilean aghmhor,
> An t-eilean grianach, mu'n iath an saile;
> Eilean buadh-mhor nam fuar-bheann arda,
> Nan coilltean uaine 'snan cluaintean fasail
>
> *The isle of Mull is of isles the fairest*
> *Of ocean gems 'tis the first and rarest,*
> *Green grassy island of sparkling fountains,*
> *Of waving woods and high tow'ring mountains.*

The verse quoted above comes from what is the veritable anthem of Mull – *The Isle of Mull* – composed by Dugald MacPhail (1818–87), one of Mull's many great men of music and story. It is as true today as when it was written

MAPS AND PICTURES

Here is some practical advice for a first visit: exploring paths and places will be so much more easy and interesting if you have a good map – Bartholomew's 1/2in to the mile (1:25,000), or for greater detail, the 1in (1:50,000) Ordnance Survey which shows old drove roads, archaeological sites and of course the contours of the high hills. A camera is a must, an indispensable medium for reviving memories in the days to come; and be sure you have plenty of film, for sometimes you find a picture awaiting round every bend of the road. Detailed advice is available at the tourist office in the busy main street in Tobermory, or you might like to inquire earlier, at the main office in Oban; Caledonian-MacBrayne can be contacted at its head office at Gourock Pier, Renfrewshire, or at the various ferry piers.

The Isle of Mull and Iona Pipe Band opening the Highland Games, Tobermory

Left: Ben More across Loch Scridain from Pennyghael

Major General Macquarie's mausoleum

FAMOUS MEN OF MULL

General Macquarie is only one of many distinguished men with Mull connections. Niall Mhor (Big Neil) was the grandfather of Dr David Livingstone, the great African missionary-explorer, and he was also a farmer in Ulva. In 1752 James Stewart, 'James of the Glen' had been vindictively arrested, tried 'By a Campbell Court and a Campbell Judge' at Inveraray, convicted and executed for the murder of Colin Campbell of Glenure, a deed of which he was totally innocent. Big Neil and his brother outwitted the soldier guarding the remains of James Stewart at Ballachulish, secretly and reverently interred them, and hurled the gibbet into the sea. They then fled to Ulva. Big Neil's grandson, Dr Livingstone, was born at Blantyre after the family left Ulva.

in distant Newcastle over a century ago. Mull is indeed unique among the Isles of the Hebrides: while other islands have just one or two individual features, in Mull, conveniently situated as it is in relation to the mainland, all features are present – and in addition it has others which are found nowhere else in the Hebridean islands, or even beyond. Perhaps the mountains lack the climbers' crags of Skye, but they are more rounded, more kindly, yet spectacularly high: Ben More (3,169ft/966m) is the highest peak of tertiary lavas in Britain, and the only 'Munro' in the Hebrides other than in Skye.

Mull is also distinguished by the fact that it is commemorated on the maps of Britain's former colonies and dominions more generously than any other part of the British Isles: in Australia, for instance, Major-General Lachlan Macquarie was the governor of New South Wales between 1810 and 1821; his father was a small farmer in the island of Ulva, which is separated from Mull by a crossing of only a few hundred yards, and during his time in office General Macquarie explored and developed the Australian province and thirled it to Mull by a selection of nostalgic place-names. On his retirement in 1821 he returned to his native island where he had earlier bought the estate of Gruline, which he re-named Jarvisfield after his wife's name. He is buried together with members of his family in the private mausoleum near Gruline House.

Mull also has a long-standing connection with the Maclean family: in 1911 Sir Fitzroy Donald Maclean, 10th Baronet of Duart and chief of the clan Maclean, who had fought in the Crimean War, purchased the castle of Duart – traditionally this was the ancestral home of the chief of the Macleans, but it had lapsed from Maclean ownership for the previous 220 years. More recently, in 1971, the former Sir Charles Maclean was raised to the peerage and became Lord Chamberlain to the Royal Household. He was also Lord Lieutenant of Argyll, and was formerly Chief Scout, and during his extensive travelling in that office he carried the name of Mull into almost every corner of the world.

There is an impressive list of men who have made the island of Mull famous, from the aristocracy, the renowned Beaton doctors of the Middle Ages, the flamboyant chiefs of their day, to the simple composers and storytellers whose works never die. Mull was always a military place, too: during the Napoleonic wars, before the population was so cruelly reduced, no fewer than 116 officers served in the army and navy, headed by five generals and an admiral – the rank and file must have made a formidable army.

But let us look at Mull as it is today. Strategically situated about halfway up the west coast of Scotland, it lies ten miles from mainland Oban, which is a natural road centre – forty minutes from Craignure in Mull by the ferry taking 1,000 passengers, 100 cars. It has many unique features: first and foremost is its geology, which has made it one of the most researched areas in the world; then, on quite a different level, it has the only passenger railway in the Hebrides, even if it is of only $10^{1}/_{4}$in gauge and runs for under two miles. It is also a highly popular link between Craignure and Torosay Castle, a splendid mansion house with extensive gardens, that attracts thousands of visitors.

For several years Mull has been the venue for one of Britain's most spectacular car rallys, attracting an entry of 120 motor cars annually in early October. This too is unique, for certain stages are run over public roads which are officially closed to the public and the Road Traffic Acts temporarily suspended. It is run by the 2300 motor and motorcycle car club ('MMCCC') of Blackburn, under rigorously strict safety and social conditions: the only stretch of main roads in Great Britain where a motorist can legally exceed 70mph! Incidentally, it is a valuable late season addition to the tourist economy of the island.

In April there is the Mull Music Festival, which from small beginnings has blossomed into one of the most popular events in the Southern Hebrides. One of the highlights of the West of Scotland yachting calendar is the annual race from the Clyde via Tarbert to the popular yachting centre of Tobermory, held in mid-July, about the same time as the Tobermory Highland Games. August sees the Mull & Morvern Agricultural Show, the oldest established event in Mull, overlooked by the ruins of old Aros Castle, at Salen, on the Sound of Mull.

Then there is the story of the Spanish galleon sunk in Tobermory Bay: this has attracted nearly fifty expeditions since the 1600s, all hoping to recover the vast treasure said to have been carried in the ship. Also of note – though now no more than a memory – is the fact that Tobermory Bay was the most vital and successful training centre in the British Isles for anti-submarine warfare during World War II. About 1,000 ships up to destroyer category and 250,000 men successfully endured the inspired and unorthodox training under Vice Admiral Sir Gilbert Stephenson, KBE, CB, CMG. The redoubtable admiral (known familiarly as 'Puggy', 'Monkey', or 'Monkey Brand') was knighted in 1943 for his immense contribution to the war effort.

We have mentioned only a few of Mull's unique interests and personalities. As you explore the island and get to know its people you will fall under its spell, and like so many visitors, return time after time until you find yourself a member of a close-knit community. Many newcomers, in fact, have settled in the island, restoring old buildings or sad ruins from a past age, choosing to enjoy the tranquillity of life in such an environment.

Before we take you round the island and point out its most interesting features, it may be helpful to describe how it was formed, its wildlife, the history of its people and the impact of Christianity – and much more besides, all of which will surely kindle fresh interest, and broaden your understanding of what you see.

The Isle of Mull railway, Craignure, with the ferry in the background

PILLAR BOXES

People interested in Post Office memorabilia will be interested to know that at the time of writing, Tobermory still uses two of the familiar red pillar boxes bearing the Royal reference 'Edward VIII'. What prompted the Post Office to install these in remote Tobermory when only a few hundred were manufactured and distributed around Britain?

1 THE GEOLOGY AND STRUCTURE OF MULL

A MEMOIR issued by the Geological Survey of Scotland in 1924 begins: 'It may safely be maintained that Mull includes the most complicated igneous centre as yet accorded detailed examination anywhere in the world.' The unravelling of the geological story of the island started over two hundred years ago.

The island of Mull is now a worn-down land surface composed of large sheets of lava which form a widely spread, thick covering over the worn-down Caledonian rocks. At the start of the Tertiary Age, Mull became one of the active volcanic centres that erupted in a great curve extending from the Mountains of Mourne in Ireland across the Hebrides and beyond. During the next ten million years, as a result of intermittent volcanic outpourings from the central and lesser vents, and from great cracks or 'dykes' as we now know them, Mull came to constitute an area of piled-up lavas that stretched far beyond its present shoreline; in time these became massively eroded, and were heavily glaciated during the later Ice Ages, to form the present landscape.

The massive glacier from the Great Glen which moved down Loch Linnhe crossed the eastern end of Mull, and rocks are found here that have been carried from the distant hills of the mainland. A branch of the glacier moved along the Sound of Mull. Glen More is another typical glaciated valley. At the watershed, innumerable erratics litter the land surface, together with moraine mounds; and on the shores at the head of Loch Scridain and Loch na Keal and elsewhere, flat rocks are heavily scored with the passing of ice-borne rocks. As the last Ice Age ended about twelve thousand years ago and the last of the ice and glaciers vanished, the landscape was left much as we see it today.

The general direction of coasts, glens and lochs still conforms roughly to similar features on the mainland, mostly running north-east to south-west following structural movements and lines of weakness that occurred during the Caledonian period. The line of the Great Glen, or Caledonian Fault, crosses Scotland from the Moray Firth, continues through Loch Linnhe and cuts across the south-east corner of Mull through Loch Spelve and Loch Buie, pushed somewhat out of line by the gigantic earth movements of the volcanic complex in central Mull. Another major feature

GLACIATION IN MULL

There are textbook examples of glaciation in Mull. The mountainous centre had its own glaciers that smoothed the rough landscape, turning rugged glens into typical 'U'-shaped, smooth-sided cross-sections. Of these, Glen Clachaig is an excellent example. It runs south-west from Loch Ba, and in former times a much-used path, still used as a right of way, ascended the glen, crossed the shoulder of Ben More and descended to Glen More near the head of Loch Scridain. Many moraine mounds lie at the mouth of the glen beside Loch Ba, and erratics (ice-borne rocks) lie everywhere they were dropped from the receding front of the glacier as it melted. Loch Ba is in fact a water-filled valley cut off from Loch na Keal by vast deposits of pebbles and glacial detritus.

Left: Across Loch Scridain from Killiemore, with Corra-Bheinn, the highest peak, on the horizon

The Island of Iona from Fionnphort

known as the Moine Thrust Plane extends south-south-west from just east of Cape Wrath, continuing under the sea until, it is thought, it passes through the Sound of Iona. Iona lies west of this line and differs geologically from Mull in that it consists very largely of extremely ancient rocks, Lewisian Gneiss, part of the great plate that extends through the Outer Hebrides across the north Atlantic. It is estimated to be 1,500 million years old and is among the oldest rocks in the world. Reference will be made later to the remarkable awareness of local people long ago to this 'permanence' of the island of Iona.

Intervals of thousands of years occurred between lava flows, long enough for the surface of earlier flows to weather down, the land to be broken up into valleys, soil to gather and vegetation to flourish, until it was all submerged by the next flow. Evidence of this appears in the small shallow seams of coal exposed west of Carsaig and at Ardtun, the leaves and flowers of sub-tropical shrubs (the fossil leaf-beds at Ardtun) preserved in mudstone, and certain tree-forms appearing below the cliffs of Burg, Ardmeanach, and at Quinish, near Dervaig.

Mull divides naturally into three areas and parishes: the north, Kilninian and Kilmore, is divided from the central mountainous area by the wide, three-mile long valley running from Salen on the Sound of Mull to the head of Loch na Keal on the west side. A line roughly from the head of Loch Scridain to Loch Buie divides the centre, Torosay, from the long peninsula ending in the Ross of Mull – Kilfinichen and Kilviceon. 'Ross' is the Gaelic word 'Ros', meaning peninsula or promontory. The three areas are so dissimilar that they are dealt with individually.

CENTRAL MULL: THE MOUNTAIN CORE

THIS IS A SPECTACULAR region of high jutting mountains and deep glens associated with the volcanic centre at the head of Loch Ba; apart from Ben More ('The Big Hill'), the highest peaks rise to 2,512ft (766m) in Dun da Ghaoithe. The area extends westwards into the bold 1,800ft (550m) plateau above Gribun, and on to the 1,000ft (305m) cliffs of the headland of Burg, in Ardmeanach. Ben More – 3,169ft (966m) – is on the western perimeter of the volcanic centre and is the highest peak of tertiary basalts in Britain, with an estimated thickness of 3,000ft (915m) of basalts. It had eroded

Calgary Bay

Creag Mhór: Gribun cliffs above Loch na Keal, from the east

massively from a maximum elevation which may have been 7,000 to 8,000ft (2,000 to 2,500m) down to its present height. Looking across Loch Scridain from the south, a viewer can clearly trace the horizontal edges of successive lava flows along the steep hill slopes of the Ardmeanach peninsula.

Gribun, on the south side of Loch na Keal, is a specially interesting area for exploration by geologists, for along the shore and exposed in the lower cliffs there are outcrops of the sedimentary rocks, some of them fossiliferous, as mentioned earlier. This unusual formation was exposed through some uplift in the coastal zone during volcanic action.

Ben Chasgidle – 1,652ft (497m) – beside Glen Cannel is the eroded core of the great volcano from which, at the beginning of the Tertiary Age, a vast quantity of basic consistency (that is, free-flowing) lavas, hardening into fine-grained basalts, poured out and built up to great heights over a wide area, with periods of quiescence between the flows. Later in the Tertiary period further activity of a different volcanic source began: the Ben Chasgidle volcano was replaced by a second and overlapping vent situated about a mile to the north, at the head of Loch Ba, now worn down level with the glen. This time the lava was of a more viscous nature and was ejected explosively to form coarse-grained rocks such as granite and gabbro. The crater of the double volcano may have been five miles in diameter.

At the end of the Tertiary Age, about 50 million years ago, an area of massive subsidences surrounded by a complex ring of dykes was left, filled from below as the central core subsided; this has attracted geologists the world over to unravel the story.

Centred on this complex is what is known as the 'Mull Swarm' of dykes stretching from the centre in a wide curve towards the south-east, one in particular extending to the Yorkshire coast, the 'Whin Sill'. Throughout the island, dykes and sills (horizontal infilled fissures) are common. Dykes of a harder consistency than the surrounding rocks stand out like walls; conversely, the softer dykes wear down into long hollows. There is an excellent example of a dyke stretching up the slope from the old pier at Calgary whose continuation can be traced on the south side of the bay. Later dykes and vents broke through earlier lava flows, such as the hill 'S Airde Ben, above the Mishnish lochs in north Mull, a minor vent now 959ft (292m) with a crater loch.

MULL'S TOPOGRAPHY

The suffix '-nish' appearing in place-names in the north of Mull – such as Mishnish, Quinish and so on – indicates an isolated flat plateau, and the name of the island itself, Mull, implies a higher, wider tableland, best understood when the island is viewed from the sea, as happened when the Vikings used and named such landmarks as sailing directions. As you take the road from Tobermory to Dervaig you will see a skyline of steps and stairs as it were, and Loch Torr, that delightful artificial angling loch halfway to Dervaig, is in fact called after the distinctive little 'tor' standing above the road at its eastern end.

NORTH MULL: THE TABLELANDS

THIS REGION IS SEPARATED from the central area by Loch na Keal (this is really 'Cille', a chapel or cell of the missionaries who spread from Iona). Similarly Loch Tuath, the North Loch, cuts into the west coast and has almost isolated the island of Ulva, necessitating a ferry crossing of just a few hundred yards. It is an area of flat boggy moorland, rising to the terraced uplands and isolated flat-topped hills ('mesas') of trap country, of which Mull is a perfect example (the word comes from the Swedish *trappa*, a step). The hills rise to no more than 1,456ft (444m) in Speinne Mor, which rises above Mull's longest freshwater loch, Loch Frisa, four miles in length. There are bold headlands and cliffs along the northern and western coasts.

All these tablelands and small isolated plateaux are the eroded remnants of the horizontal lava sheets that spread far beyond the whole area, and cut back so slowly that the time it took them to change passes our comprehension.

Around Loch na Keal, along the Sound of Mull and in other localities, raised beaches are a feature, especially the 25ft beach which is backed by old

sea cliffs and caves. These raised beaches were formed when the whole land surface was rising as a result of losing its burden of ice at the end of the Ice Age, and the loss of heavy deposits of volcanic materials by erosion over the ages; for of course the surface of the earth is like an elastic cover over its molten interior. The land surface could also have been affected by earth movements associated with volcanic activities.

THE ROSS OF MULL

THE EASTERN END of this long peninsula is covered by lava flows to a height of 1,500ft (455m); the surface slopes up gently from the shores of Loch Scridain to the continuous line of high cliffs on the southern shore. West of Bunessan there is a low area of worn-down ancient crystalline rocks, and west of Loch Lathaich are the famous red and pink granites. There are some fine sandy beaches in the south-west.

The uniform stretch of high cliffs on the south coast is broken by the picturesque bay of Carsaig, with its amphitheatre of 700ft (215m) cliffs towering above a small, fertile, grassy plain, below which is a curving beach of dark basaltic sand. Fossiliferous sediments outcrop west of the bay; but of even greater interest is the outcrop of lignite coal on the lower slopes of the hill just south of Carsaig Bay. This deposit and the small associated patches occurring between the lava sheets indicate the existence at one time of sub-tropical conditions.

Caves above the Carsaig shoreline are associated with a higher sea level (as found elsewhere in Mull), caves such as the Nuns' Cave a mile west of the bay, the spectacular Carsaig Arches beyond, and Lord Lovat's Cave near Lochbuie, another break in the cliffs above which the fertile plain 'the Magh' has given its name to Moy Castle there.

More evidence of changing conditions is to be found in the well-known 'leaf-beds' of Ardtun, near Bunessan, an accumulation of fossil

The Nuns' Cave

Left: Carsaig Arches

19

Columnar basalt cliffs on Staffa

leaves and petals in a layer of mudstone lying between early lava flows. The leaves must have fallen autumn after autumn into the still waters of a shallow lake, on whose muddy bottom they accumulated in layers, fully expanded and undisturbed. The mudstone can be split into thin plates, and botanical examination has shown that the leaves were from trees now found in sub-tropical conditions: ginko, sequoia and various conifers.

COLUMNAR BASALT

NOWHERE IN BRITAIN are such spectacular and well-known examples of columnar basalt found as in Mull. This formation is confined to the earliest lava flows, and also, to judge from the distribution, in the western area. The best examples are seen on the island of Staffa ('Pillar Island'), but the extensive stretch of the south-east shoreline of Ulva (known as 'The Castle'), although less well known, is almost as arresting. Elsewhere, columnar basalts are found in the Carsaig cliffs, in the National Trust area known as the Wilderness, on the wild headland of Ardmeanach, and in the Carsaig Arches; and there are less spectacular and rudimentary forms in most parts of the island.

Columnar formations were created by the cooling and contracting process of lava: as the lava outpourings began to cool, their upper faces would lose heat more rapidly than the base which cooled more slowly and regularly. This led to regular contracting and jointing at right-angles to the cooling surfaces, and the resultant columns are usually hexagonal, although sometimes they may have from three to eight sides. This conforms to Nature's rule on economising space: for example, if a bundle of cigarettes is squeezed, each one contracts into a hexagonal, or honeycomb, pattern with its neighbours.

When the columns are curved it shows that the cooling surfaces were not parallel to each other and that the columns were obliged to bend in an effort to conform to the right-angle rule. The most spectacular examples of this are at the Clamshell Cave and Buchaille Rock in Staffa, and the immediate surrounds of fossil trees in Ardmeanach.

Contractions sometimes squeezed certain constituents, such as calcite, out of the basalt to make fine vertical joints, as if the columns were cemented together.

McCulloch's Tree

DR MCCULLOCH was the first to describe, in 1819, the 'Fossil Tree of Burgh', regarded by geologists of the 1924 Geological Survey in their memoir on Mull as 'the most arresting single geological formation in the island'; it is, in fact, one of the natural wonders of Europe. It is the cast of an ancient coniferous tree trunk, 40ft (12m) high, embedded in the lowest lava flow of the cliffs at Rudha nan Uamha (Point of the Caves), a hundred yards north of the double waterfall of Allt Airidh nan Chaisteal, the most westerly point of Ardmeanach.

When the first spread of lava flowed across the ancient land surface that was covered with forests, McCulloch's tree was engulfed, yet it exerted just enough cooling influence and resistance with its sappy bulk (it is nearly 5ft (1.5m) in diameter) to preserve its outline in the solidifying flow. The lowest 3ft (90cm) of the trunk survived, fossilised by siliceous water, and the original grain of the wood can be traced on the surface. In a cavity at the side a quantity of the original charcoal is still to be seen – at least, what is left of it after 'souvenirs' have been inadvisedly removed by visitors. It is apparently as fresh as when the tree was charred by the great heat millions of years ago.

The local cooling influence of the bulk of the tree modified the vertical jointing pattern of the surrounding columnar basalt, which is curved from the vertical to the horizontal within the last 3ft (90cm) of the trunk. Over the ages the cliff has been cut back until the vertical cross-section of the tree remains exposed, and looking down on to the flat shore from the approach path, the observer will see at one point horizontal 'cart-wheel' formations on

McCulloch's Tree (Photo: Author)

the flat worn rocks – it can be speculated that these are what remain of the base of tree trunks with the distorted columns radiating from the cooling centre like spokes of a wheel.

The walk to the tree will be described later (see p79), but those who tackle the sheep and wild goat paths along the glacis of the cliffs are advised to arrive at the tree at half-tide or on a falling tide, otherwise they face the risk of being cut off for hours at the base of the cliff. In fact the National Trust for Scotland, which owns this area – known as the Wilderness – advises visitors to call at Burg Farm, the last farm to be reached on the way, where they should report their intention to visit the tree and obtain directions.

Erosion of a raised beach near Scarisdale

THE QUINISH TREE

IN 1984 a peculiar pipe or column of rock was discovered on the rocky shore below high-water mark near Quinish Point, in the extreme north of Mull, by Tommy Maclean, member of an old Dervaig family. He described it to me, and I examined and photographed it and sent details, with rock specimens, to the Hunterian Museum (Department of Geology) in Glasgow, and to the British Geological Survey in Edinburgh. It is their opinion that this is indeed an important discovery, and that a fossil tree has been found in a new area of Mull.

It is the cast of the trunk of a tree 24ft (7.3m) in length by 20in (50cm) in diameter, cut through at one point by a narrow fracture or geological dyke that has displaced 3ft (90cm) of the trunk. Further exploration of the site revealed several smaller stumps protruding from beds of ash or tuff, and three metres from the original tree there is the long outline of another tree deeply embedded. All of them are lying in a line from north-east to south-west; unlike McCulloch's tree, which was massive enough to remain upright in the flow.

An interesting theory is that trees growing in this area were on the line of a violent eruptive blast, and there is evidence of this from the volcanic centre in Ben Hiant, across the Sound of Mull in Ardnamurchan, seven miles (11km) to the north-east. Their sappy wooden content resisted the covering of ash and tuff – such rock, and not lava, predominates in the immediate vicinity – though in time this woody content disintegrated, leaving open pipes; lava was then injected into these from below under immense pressure from an adjoining dyke or dykes, which being of a harder chemical nature than the surrounding rock resisted the massive erosion of following centuries and left casts of the trees as we see them today. Such dykes cut through the earlier flows, but may not have reached the surface of the last lava flow.

It is possible that the Quinish trees grew on the weathered surface of an early lava flow between periods of volcanic activity, before being over-whelmed. And it could well be that this horizon extended over the whole area, and that McCulloch's tree, the Ardtun leaf-beds, and the Quinish tree were contemporary, and were simultaneously covered by renewed volcanic activity. Widespread forests may have grown then, as they did since the post-Ice Age.

GEOLOGY IN THE ECONOMY OF MULL

OF COURSE, Mull has an unlimited supply of rocks of all textures, much used in the local buildings, houses, piers and jetties, and in the hundreds of miles of drystone walls. Within a hundred years of the Enclosures Act of the eighteenth century, ten thousand miles of such walls had been built in Scotland, from the 6ft march walls of the estates to the standard 4ft 6in. Beside the roads you will notice many of those tiny old quarries for the extraction of different grades of road materials, for the roadmen were skilled in the right selections.

In the Fionnphort/Assapol district of the Ross of Mull, the pink or red Ross of Mull granite was very much in demand for forty years up to the beginning of the twentieth century; only then, because of competition from mainland granites, did the industry decline. From the Ross quarries thousands of tons were shipped around the world, particularly to North America. Very attractive curling stones of this granite were in use for many years, but the texture proved to be rather soft for the harsh treatment received in the course of playing the 'Roaring Game', and they were replaced by the harder, close-grained, but drab granites from Wales and Ailsa Craig in the Firth of Clyde.

As an interesting aside we suggest that an enterprising diver may find several of the red granite stones on the bottom of Loch Pellach, the 'Bottom Loch' of the Mishnish lochs near Tobermory, about fifty yards off the shore under ten feet of water. They had been left on the ice long ago during one of Mull's rare hard frosts, when a sudden thaw melted the ice.

THE 'IONA PEBBLE'

Visitors to Iona will soon be familiar with the 'Iona pebble': these beautifully coloured stones, only an inch or two in length, are cast up by the action of the waves on the south and west shores of the island. A green variety of serpentine, they are soft enough to be worked into tiny curios and ornaments. The pebbles are probably nodules washed out of an under-sea extension of the Iona marble.

This fine white marble exists in a 40ft (12m) stratum running north-north-west to south-south-east at the south-east corner of the island. It cuts easily, is durable, and polishes well, although it tends to yellow with age. Late in the eighteenth century the marble was quarried extensively, but demand tapered off and little work has been done since the beginning of the twentieth century. The quarry could be brought into production if a new demand arose, and it can be readily inspected, being an easy walk from Iona village.

In early times, certainly in 1688 as reported by that indefatigable traveller Sacheverell, governor of the Isle of Man, a great block of marble 6 by 4ft (1.8 by 1.2m) was serving as an altar in Iona Cathedral. However, it disappeared piecemeal because of the superstition among fishermen that a piece of the altar carried in their boats averted shipwreck.

Right: Ardmeanach as seen across Loch na Lathàich

The main quarry is at Tormore, quite near Fionnphort. It stands a few hundred yards inland above a lovely beach of white sand, where there is a crumbling jetty to which a tramway ran down to deliver the material for shipment. Large stockpiles of blocks still lay in the quarry until recently, some as long as 10ft (3m) and up to 3ft (1m) square. All the work was done by hand. Originally the method of splitting the granite was to insert wooden wedges into the cracks (it splits evenly into horizontal slabs) and to expand the wood by constantly soaking it with water. This time-wasting procedure was superseded by the 'plug and feathers' method introduced from the Mourne quarries in Ireland in 1860, whereby a line of holes was drilled, each hole $1^1/_2$ in (38mm) in diameter and all 6in (15cm) apart; two metal wedges – the 'feathers' – were then inserted into each hole, and an iron wedge – the 'plug' – driven between the feathers' smooth walls – when hammered in turn, an even pressure was exerted which split the granite along the line of holes.

The large blocks were used for such massive building works as docks, bridges and harbour works; Skerryvore and Dhuheartach lighthouses that lie in the open sea west and south of Mull were built with these. The Prince Consort monument in Hyde Park, London, was also built partly of Mull granite, as were Blackfriars Bridge and Holborn Viaduct; so too were Liverpool Docks and Jamaica Bridge in Glasgow – to mention only a few. Its attractive appearance and high polish made it popular for facings on many public buildings.

Distance, transport and difficulty of access inhibit the exploitation of such materials as the hard, grey, Carsaig sandstones, which also appear north of Tobermory. The Carsaig sandstone was actually worked up to 1873. The flat tidal levels of this rock in front of the Nuns' Cave were worked long ago by the monks of Iona, to be used as grave slabs, window facings, and for some of the ornamentation of the abbey. The same method of splitting must have been used as at Tormore, but this time the sea conveniently kept the wood soaked.

The same extraction difficulties prevent the exploitation of the highest quality silica sand out-cropping at Gribun – the same quality as the extensive and more convenient deposits at Lochaline, in Morvern. Since World War II this sand has been particularly useful in high-grade optical work.

Although peat is not a rock, it does enter into the formation of coal measures. The peat as we now know it, is an accumulation of post-glacial organic matter, laid down layer by layer under wet conditions, improving in quality (when cut and dried) the deeper it lies and the greater the compression. Peat provided an aromatic fuel for the people until coal became available at an attractive price. We recollect that a ton of coal cost ten shillings – 50p – in the early years of the twentieth century! Cutting and preparing the peat on the moors for domestic fuel was hard, tedious work and its success was dependent on drying winds: the water content of peat is so high that twenty tons as dug yield one ton of dry fuel!

Previous page: Fionnphort

2 CLIMATE, VEGETATION AND WILDLIFE

CLIMATE

MULL shares the climate of the western seaboard of Scotland, with cool summers and mild winters. The incidence of frost is negligible compared with mainland conditions, and snow, which rarely falls, soon disappears except on the northern slopes of the high hills. These circumstances reflect a combination of factors: the prevailing winds are westerly or south-westerly, and the air brought to the island has been warmed by its passage over the comparatively warm waters of the North Atlantic Drift that flows out of the Gulf Stream; hence the fairly amenable winter conditions. Also, the configuration of the island allows the penetration of warm, moist air. Conversely in summer, as the earth warms up, the surrounding waters exert a cooling influence on the land temperatures and so in very hot weather Mull benefits by its very insularity.

From early in the twentieth century summer and winter conditions have perceptibly evened out, with more persistent winds and moisture. This has had the effect of bringing about long-lasting autumns and early springs, with a noticeable effect on vegetation, for example the first flowering of certain plants comes as early in Mull as it does in, say, the Cheshire Plain or Humberside.

GHOSTLY TALES

At Sunipol House, which is situated near the edge of the cliff not far from Caliach, small stones were found mysteriously scattered round the house, and this gave rise to a local story: a former resident here long ago ran short of funds and 'took a leap' as he said in the Gaelic, out to Australia; in due course he returned with his finances more than restored – but although a proportion of the funds was obtained by some bushranging, it was also said that they were augmented by monies awarded per head of aborigines hunted down and eliminated. Those stones, the local people averred, were hurled at Sunipol House by the ghosts of the aborigines murdered by the incumbent.

Above: Grass Point, the nearest point of Mull to Oban and the mainland and former ferry point

Right: Common seals are often seen along the coast of Mull. This one at Grass Point, however, is made of stone (Photo: Author)

However, exposed as it is to the Atlantic gales, the island does receive both a large amount of rain and strong winds, and the narrow glens tend to funnel the wind into the central areas. Glen More, for instance, bare and treeless, used to have lines of telegraph poles along its lonely road, and in addition to the stout stays normally used to anchor them, in certain places the poles had to be set into foundations of logs sunk deeply into the soft bogland to prevent them being flattened to the ground or torn right out. In a severe gale, streams descending the worn clefts and chimneys of exposed sea cliffs, such as the 1,000ft cliffs of Ardmeanach, are halted and blown back like smoke over the top. At Caliach Point in the extreme north-west of Mull, quite large stones are carried on to the top of the cliffs by a combination of wind and wave, and can be seen scattered about over 100ft (30m) above sea

INSECTS

Tales about insect pests are much exaggerated. If there is any wind at all they do not appear, nor are they present on the higher hill slopes or out on the water. Under still, warm conditions they are distracting, especially in boggy surroundings and along highwater mark among old seaweeds; then the visitor is advised to take a good midge cream with him which will give protection for several hours. In Mull we do not worry about appearances, and find perfect protection from midges under even the worst of conditions by wearing a veil of very fine green nylon; this baffles them, while clegs and flies are frustrated by the simple method used by the Australian swagman – wear a broad-brimmed hat with corks suspended from the brim on lengths of nylon fishing gut: any movement sets the corks dancing, and the pests stay away!

level on ground swept bare by the wave-tops.

Mull is wetter than any of the other Hebridean islands. According to records kept at three points in Mull and one in Iona, statistics prepared in the 1980s state that the average rainfall per year varies from 81.3in (206.5cm) at Auchnacraig (near Grass Point in the extreme east), which is in the lee of the mountainous centre of the island, to 48.4in (122.9cm) in Iona. Although the latter is in the most exposed westerly position, the fact that it is so low-lying is to its advantage, because the moist air does not give up its rain until it is cooled by rising against the central mountains – on Ben More and other high places the annual rainfall reaches 125in (317.5cm), an amount equalled in the Hebrides only by a small central area in the higher and more massive Cuillins of Skye.

The average as given by rainfall records over a period of nearly forty years shows that May has normally been the driest month with only 3.66in (9.3cm); thereafter the monthly average rises to a maximum of 8.4in (21.3cm) in October. This is, of course, merely an arithmetical average for the whole island; but it shows that while rain can be expected at any time, the driest months are late spring and early summer. There are local variations in rainfall depending on such factors as height above sea level, and the character of the soil and even of the vegetation, notably the extending woodlands. Peat-covered areas are commonly waterlogged and produce locally humid conditions; sandy and well-drained areas are drier.

The moderating influence of the surrounding waters and of the North Atlantic Drift is best illustrated by the relatively small range of temperatures that Mull experiences. The difference between the averages of the warmest and the coldest months is about 9°C (16°F); it is interesting to compare this with annual ranges in the Grampians (at about the same latitude) of over 11°C (20°F) and in the Home Counties around London of over 14°C (25°F). Sea-surface temperatures around Mull (reached later in the sea than on the land) are 8°C (46°F) in winter and over 12°C (54°F) in summer; this is comparatively mild in relation to east coast temperatures at about the same latitude. Hill temperatures are of course lower, and approximately 1°F is lost for every 300ft (91m) of elevation – so many climbers and hill walkers forget this, and do not equip themselves properly to meet the colder conditions on the high hills.

The statistics quoted above are of course averages – that is, generalities. On the whole, Mull probably enjoys just as much sunshine as south-west Scotland, and in some years we have enjoyed weeks of unbroken sunshine, when from the many vantage points in Mull the Hebridean islands have stood out clearly, the colours incredibly beautiful; even the upper slopes of the hills of Harris in the Outer Hebrides, sixty miles distant, have been visible, the lower slopes hidden by the curvature of the earth. Sunsets can be spectacular, when a gentle wind comes in from the sea, and the enthusiastic angler can expect the big loch trout to come to the fly.

VEGETATION

BETWEEN 1965 AND 1970 the Department of Botany of the British Museum conducted a survey of the flora and environment of Mull: 5,280 species and varieties in over 1,600 genera, including those mentioned in all known records, were specified; this covered the 450 square miles of the island, and a similar area of the surrounding sea-bed. Obviously space permits no more than a brief review of the survey, and interested readers are strongly recommended to read its detailed findings: *The Isle of Mull: A Survey of its Flora and Environment*, published by the Department of Botany, British Museum (Natural History), edited by A. C. Jermy and J. A. Crabbe.

VISITING TIMES

The duration of sunshine is naturally related to cloudiness and of course rainfall. January and February are the coldest months, July and August the warmest; mid-July is often a wet period and rather cloudy. Certainly May and June, and late August to September are periods to be recommended for visits to the island: up to the month of June the irritating attentions of midges, clegs (horse flies) and the common house fly are absent, and the bracken has not reached its full development – in hollows and sheltered places it can reach a height of 5ft (1.5m) – when it can conceal objects of interest and also make the going harder off the beaten track. In August and September the heather is in full bloom and the early autumn colourings are superb. For the angler, salmon and sea-trout should be well established in their freshwater haunts, and brown trout are back 'on the take' after their mid-season off-period.

Harebells – the 'Scottish bluebell' near Tobermory

Left: Sunset over Ardmeanach from Pennyghael

FLORA AND FAUNA

Past or present association with man has a marked effect on plant life. Thus plants escape from cultivation and thrive in the wild, such as certain herbs grown in the Ross of Mull by the Beaton doctors in the Middle Ages. Hemlock is another example, and flax is a survivor from the days when it was actively cultivated. In Iona – a particularly rewarding island for botanists – deadly nightshade (Atropa belladonna) was a drug-plant used by the monks in the Middle Ages. Old mortared walls have a high lime content and so have their special plants – for instance, the ruined walls of the nunnery in Iona. Embankments along new roads will often have a rich new growth of white clover. Sheep, cattle, goats and deer influence soil fertility and habitat, both encouraging and destroying growth: thus sheep will sour grazing by over-use, encouraging the presence of bracken. Further, in their grazing habits they tug the grass and destroy the roots; unlike cattle, which cut rather than tug. Cattle also destroy bracken by treading it down and fertilise the ground with their droppings. Goats feed on and destroy almost everything they can reach, while deer, the enemy of the forester, ring bark and nip out the tender tops of young trees.

Right: Highland cattle in Loch Beg

Mull was chosen because of its unique situation, being a pivotal point on the west coast of Britain between the southern oceanic and the northern mountain flora, as well as for its affinity with the flora of the mainland.

Geology, the chemical composition of the rocks, and the climate all have a major effect on the flora of an area, which is also influenced by the presence of man, livestock, birds and wildlife. Many factors combine to provide such a wide variety of habitats. For instance, the high percentage of nitrates round the nesting places of sea-birds encourages abundant growth of the common sorrel (*Rumex acetosa*) and chickweed. Pignut (*Conopodium majus*) and wood sedge (*Carex sylvatica*) grow freely on old woodland sites, while former swamplands encourage the growth of reeds (*Phragmites australis*). Again, the rare Iceland purslane (*Koenigia islandica*) is found only in Mull and Skye, owing its existence to a rare balance between elevation, salt-laden winds, and rapid freezing and thawing. Another plant found in Mull, but otherwise rare in Scotland, is fool's parsley (*Aethusa cynapium*).

Nettles always spring up where man has been, even in forgotten sites far distant in the hills. One such site we have seen is situated far from the nearest dwelling – it consists of several rings of stones, scant remains of the walls of tiny habitations; these are situated in a wide area of heather, and the heather growth is particularly thick and coarse at the edge of each ring as if struggling to encroach on the grassy centre where a thick patch of nettles grows – but in vain. This shows the effect that even trace elements and nitrogen from ashes, refuse and so on, can have if left in the soil.

Rain distribution is more important than the total precipitation. There are 200 to 220 'wet' days on average, a wet day being defined as precipitation of 0.04in (1mm). Fogs and sea mists encourage lush plant growth, and on the leeward side of the island the distribution of certain species of alpine plants. About one third of alpine plants grow above the 1,000ft (305m) level. High local rainfall results in leaching of the soil, however, with long-term effects on plant growth and species.

In the boglands there is a great variety of coarse grasses, mosses and fungi; there are also many attractive species of orchid in marshy places, some of them found only in Mull. Mosses and fungi are particularly abundant on the eastern side, in the clean pollution-free atmosphere where humidity is greater and the winds have a lower salt content.

Marine plants follow much the same pattern as terrestrial; inevitably they are affected by the extent to which they are sheltered from, or exposed to ocean currents, by the geology of the sea floor, by sand, light, salinity (which is less as the coast is approached) and finally oxygen content. This is much greater where the streams flow in, thus attracting sea-trout and salmon and encouraging them to seek their upstream spawning grounds, or redds, as they are called. The freshwater lochs conform in their analysis to Scotland as a whole.

From the time Mull assumed its present form after massive erosion, soil with the chemical constituents of the underlying rocks began to gather.

Glaciation swept away the weathered surface, depositing the detritus in places protected from the main ice-stream. Subsequently the local rocks began to break down, depositing a layer of soil over the whole area. Plateau basalts (covering 45 per cent of Mull) give a brown, loamy soil very suitable for cultivation, grazing and woodlands; Mull owes its green hilltops to this type of soil, which turns to peat over hard rocks. The central mountain complex (35 per cent of Mull) consists of alluvial gravels and sandy loams; this allows some cultivation, otherwise it supports only rough grazing and forestry on the terminal moraines and alluvial deposits. Ross of Mull granite (5 per cent) yields an undulating, ridged, rocky landscape, with shallow soil and clay pockets, loam and deep peat, suitable for rough grazing and some cultivation. Schist (3 per cent) produces clay loams suitable for extensive cultivation, rough grazing and forestry. Raised beaches (4 per cent) give a gravelly sandy soil, allowing extensive cultivation and rough grazing. Organic soils contain over 20 per cent organic matter and exceed 10in (25cm) in depth; when they become waterlogged, oxygen is excluded, decomposition is restricted, and most such soils qualify as peat.

On moors and grasslands the purple moor-grass (*Molinia caerulea*) gives its typical colouring to the grasslands at an altitude of 500–1,000ft (150–305m), notably on the trap landscapes of the west and south; tussocky in nature, it dominates other species and smothers other plants. On the higher moorlands (over 1,000ft/305m) and in the more acid soils of the central area the vegetation is that associated with the fescue and bent (*Festuca agrostis*) of the sheep-grazing moors; it is poor grassland, growing better on the sandy valley moraines of the central complex.

Moorlands and the steeper slopes carry a widespread growth of ling heather (*Calluna vulgaris*), and bell heather (*Erica cinerea*) is abundant. In damper areas the cross-leaved heath (*Erica tetralix*), with its delicate fragrance, is plentiful, along with bog-myrtle. White-flowered ling ('white heather') in little clumps or single sprigs can be found by the observant searcher in young, well-established growths.

The quality of the common ling has deteriorated during the course of the twentieth century. The reasons are partly climatic and partly disease, but most of all because of the lack of rotational burning which should take place every fifteen to twenty years to create a healthy regeneration. Skilled management of heather moors is essential if they are to be used profitably as sheep or grouse lands, because both depend on young, healthy growth.

BRACKEN

Bracken (Peridium aquilinum) is the menace of the stock-raiser. It grows most freely on brown forest soils 10in (25cm) deep or deeper, and has spread extensively since the disappearance of the small agricultural units prevalent before the clearances of the land in the nineteenth century, and the widespread reduction in cattle herds. Its upper limit of growth at 1,000ft (305m) marks potential forest limits, both past and present; but in well-drained land it spreads quickly and soon smothers grasslands. Certain modern chemical sprays can be applied in August when growth is just at its most exotic and these are effective but costly eliminators. In former times, when manpower was more generally available, the growing shoots were scythed in early summer for at least three consecutive years, which discouraged growth.

THE RICHES OF NATURE

SCRAMBLING ALONG the rocky shore at low tide can be as rewarding as searching the hills for white heather, for there are so many different things to be observed – different species of seaweed, for instance, including two forms of red algae found at low tides: dulse (*Rhodymenia*) and carragheen (*Chandrus crispus*), both of which are edible, possessing a rich salty tang. There are the creatures of the rocky pools, the beauty of empty shells, the flotsam of sea life and items carried by the sea from far places. There is the artistry of the waves carved into the rocks.

Inland, the blossoms are richest in late spring and early summer. At first the woodlands are carpeted with masses of wood anemones and wood sorrel, with primroses, wild violets and hyacinths in a blue drift. This is followed by an increasing riot of wild flowers. Many species of toadstool grow among the deep mosses and on the rotting wood of old birch trees, and in the plantations the fresh green shoots of the larch trees contrast with the darker spruce. Summer has the fragrance of the fragile dog-rose and honeysuckle; everywhere in the boglands is the unforgettable scent of bog myrtle and bog-mint. Autumn brings the purple of the heather, blending with the rich colours of the dying bracken fronds. Wild fruits are plentiful, especially brambles (blackberries), wild raspberries and strawberries, the last often growing to the size of a large hazelnut with an acid sweetness more delicious than that of the cultivated varieties. In early October hazelnuts are plentiful, especially in south-facing hazel thickets. From then onwards, when the sap is low, is the time for rhabdophilists – an impressive name for the artists of crook and stick-making – to search the hazel thickets for suitable blocks and shafts of hazel which will provide an absorbing winter hobby: transforming the crude materials into sticks for casual use with intricate ornamentation; or into plain, stout crooks for the practical use of stock-raisers.

WILDLIFE

THE LARGEST NATIVE MAMMAL in Mull is the red deer, in number estimated at about three thousand head. Except during the hard winter months they are found high up in the hills and concentrated in the sporting estates of Torosay, Ben More 'forest' (from *Foresta* in fact meaning a rough open landscape), and in the Laggan peninsula. They become something of a nuisance when they come down from the hills to nibble growing crops or to browse the young trees in new plantations. Commercial deer farming is a possibility, but it would depend on such factors as having sufficient acres to carry a viable herd, and being able to provide the extra staffing and capital expenditure needed for the handling, storing and exporting of carcases. There is a herd of fallow deer in the woodlands around Knock and Gruline, while roe deer are also present.

BLACK MINK

In December 1993 a letter in the local paper, the weekly Oban Times, described the increasing problem of black mink in the Highlands. A few years ago some Animal Rights people – ill-advised and apparently heedless of the lesson to be learned elsewhere – released a number of these black predators in the Morvern area. The destruction they have caused is deplorable, particularly in bird colonies along the Sound of Mull; moreover as they are excellent swimmers it is almost inevitable that they will spread across to Mull, an invasion which will lead to havoc among wildlife, especially birds, and disturb the balance of nature in this natural conservation island. Mink in the wild are vermin and efforts should be made to exterminate them.

Left: Red deer grazing at Grass Point, with Lismore in the distance

RABBIT STEW

Rabbits were a useful, albeit monotonous, addition to the islanders' diet, and furthermore were profitably exported to the mainland. However there is the story of a visiting minister who, after a meal of stewed rabbit, called on the man of the house to give thanks after eating; in fact the words of the crofter's grace feelingly summed up his attitude to rabbits:

Rabbits young and rabbits old;
Rabbits hot and rabbits cold;
Rabbits tender and rabbits tough,
I thank the Lord I've had enough.

MULL ADDERS

An adder will only ever strike a defensive pose if it is cornered, or when torpid in hot weather with young nearby. The largest adders we have seen in Mull measured 32in (81cm), but the average length is about 24in (61cm) for an adult. The effective striking distance of a coiled-up adder has been proved by experiment never to exceed 10–12in (25–30cm). They like to frequent the margins of lochs and marshy places where frogs, their favourite food, are most abundant. One of the most fascinating observations of an adder that we have had was of a small specimen which had coiled itself round a branch projecting over a tiny woodland stream and which was sipping the water underneath with a bird-like motion. There is no doubt at all that Mull adders are timid, and any reputation for ferocity is just a story.

Both brown and blue hares are resident, the blue hare growing a white coat for the winter. They were unaffected by the disease myxomatosis which in the 1950s almost wiped out the hordes of Mull rabbits that lived in the confines of burrows rather than in the open, like hares. Rabbits have existed in Mull since the Middle Ages and at one time increased to a point where their habits presented a serious threat to livestock grazings. In fact on one hill farm in Mull the farmer was able to increase his stock of grazing cattle by fifty per cent once myxomatosis had taken its toll of the rabbits. Unfortunately they are on the increase again.

Moles appeared as recently as the 1880s when a pair is said to have been accidentally brought over in a load of earth ballast from Morvern. Stoats and weasels are common, and the pole-cat – sometimes confused with ferrets that have escaped and bred in the wilds – was reported to have reappeared in the 1950s. Wild goats frequent the high cliffs at Ardmeanach and along the south coast of Mull, descendants of the domestic goats that either escaped or were turned loose at the time of the Clearances.

Field mice, wood mice, voles, shrews, and of course rats are all common in Mull. Otters are common along the shores and beside certain lochs and rivers, but their number is at a steady level and presents no problem. True, they do take a toll of trout and salmon, but their favourite food is the eel. All along the shores of Mull and especially along the Sound of Mull, the common seal can usually be observed; while on the Treshnish Islands there is a breeding ground for grey seals on the rocky platforms just above sea level, where they gather from the month of August onwards. Unlike the otter, the seal can be a menace to the stake nets of salmon fishers along the coast. A single seal can destroy hundreds of pounds' worth of nets and be the cause of countless escaped or mangled salmon, all at any one time, and in such a precarious economy this can impose considerable financial strain on salmon fishermen. The number of seals must therefore not be allowed to increase.

Moths, butterflies, beetles and all the commoner insects are widespread; we have already described midges, clegs (horse flies) and house flies. In the sometimes warm, moist, windless conditions during the summer there is a vast amount of insect life, from ephemeridae to dragon and damsel flies in boglands and around the margins of lochs. When a hatch of insects takes place – their life only a matter of hours before they mate and die – the surface of the water often has a skin of dead insects, and trout become too gorged to show any interest in the anglers' lures.

Mull has its share of reptiles and amphibians – frogs, newts, toads and (infrequently) leeches . In hot weather tiny lizards sun themselves, and you may be aware of slow-worms and adders, the only species of snake found on the island. In fact adders are seldom seen because they are timid and vanish at the vibration of a footfall; if approached very quietly they may be observed basking on sun-warmed rocks and mossy walls, even on the top of bracken and tussocks of moor grass.

Lunga, with the Dutchman's Cap on the horizon

Above: Fulmar in flight, below: Puffin

BIRDLIFE

THE GREAT VARIETY of birdlife in and around the island attracts huge numbers of enthusiastic ornithologists to Mull; and remember that, however keen you are, a pair of good binoculars will undoubtedly bring a new dimension to the study of wildlife. According to an authoritative count, 203 different species of birds have been seen in Mull, from the wren to the golden and sea eagles. Some are rarely seen, many are resident all the year round, but most of them can be observed during particular seasons: at breeding times, when they are wintering on the island, or when they are just passing through to another destination. For full information it is suggested that those interested should contact the British Trust for Ornithology, or the Scottish Ornithological Club (21 Regent Terrace, Edinburgh).

Probably the golden eagle is the most impressive bird in the island and it is now becoming fairly numerous, nesting in some of the more inaccessible corners; its great wing-span and magnificent soaring habits are unmistakable, and a source of admiration. The sea eagle (or white-tailed eagle) has been re-introduced to the Hebrides, several pairs having been brought over each year from Scandinavia to the isle of Rum; it is now quite a common sight around the north of Mull. Both the golden and the sea eagles gained the

THE TRESHNISH ISLANDS

Perhaps the best of the birdlife around Mull is to be seen on the Treshnish Islands, a natural bird sanctuary, in late spring and early summer. Regular visits to these islands are included in the interesting programmes offered in day cruises from the various centres in Mull, and it is no exaggeration to say they are amongst the most fascinating. Here there are established colonies of the many varieties of gull, also of puffins, guillemots, shag and cormorant (called 'scart'

locally, from the Gaelic scarabh) and still other species – the cliffs echo with their noisy clamour, the ground is littered with rough untidy nests, while any grassy spot houses burrows of puffins, the clown among them all, its parrot bill usually with a moustache of sandeels draped across it; but wonderful swimmers. Rocks and cliffs are whitened with their droppings. Nor are these the only representatives: wild geese often halt here to browse on the rich grass beyond the congested cliff-tops.

Above: Razorbills; opposite: Guillemots

exaggerated reputation of being predators of livestock, especially of young lambs, which in fact has rarely been evidenced. Consequently the sea eagle was harried to extinction here before the 1880s, and the golden eagle just missed the same fate; in his book *100 Years in the Highlands* the late Osgood Mackenzie described how in Wester Ross during the mid-nineteenth century the killing of two pairs of nesting golden eagles in a day was a welcome achievement.

There are numerous buzzards, though these are often mistaken for the golden eagle; however, comparison shows up their smaller size and lower flight, and the way in which they are often seen perching prominently on the lookout for prey. Other birds of prey include the sparrow hawk, kestrel, merlin, peregrine and the hen harrier. Nor must we forget that cunning member of the crow family, the hooded or 'hoodie' crow, which is hated by farmers and shot on sight (if it can be approached near enough) for its habit of attacking the eyes and underbelly of sheep and lambs weakened or helpless at lambing time caught fast in bogs or briars.

Cuckoos find Mull an ideal place for their attentions, and we have counted as many as seven or eight within a quarter-mile stretch of woodland, each with its slave attendant, a meadow pipit. Also Mull is within the only area in Great Britain where the corncrake appears to have survived, and its harsh cry can still be heard, albeit infrequently. Loss of its natural habitat through intensive farming and modern clearances in the countryside have led to its extinction in so many places.

The native grouse used to be fairly plentiful in Mull; but sadly their coveys are now rarely seen. It lives on the flowers of the heather, and as we have described, most of this has become coarse, woody, and above the reach of feeding birds. This state of affairs prevails because the moor is not managed properly with a view to conserving game: estate management costs became too high, and perhaps there was a certain falling-off in interest. Without gamekeepers, predators proliferate; with no programme of controlled burning, there is nothing for the birds to eat. Pheasants – not an indigenous species – are reared on some estates, for instance on Torosay, where they are numerous in the woodlands and shrubberies through which the little railway from Craignure passes. Blackcock have died out in Mull, though Ptarmigan, which don their white plumage in winter, sometimes fly across from the mainland to the tops of Dun da Ghaoithe and adjacent hills.

In the hill lochs great northern divers and mergansers take their toll of trout, and an angler need hardly bother to set up his tackle if one of these wary birds has been there before him scaring the fish. Along the shores the piping call of oyster-catchers – St Brigid's Bird – and redshanks echoes back from the rocks and cliffs; and shags and cormorants stand tall on the offshore reefs with outstretched wings, basking in the sunshine, their crops replete with fish.

3 THE PEOPLING OF THE ISLANDS

THE EARLY SETTLERS

BETWEEN 5000 and 3000 years BC the environment had so improved that it attracted nomadic hunter-fisher groups, or 'strand-loopers' as they are called. However, those caves where they sheltered are now no longer on the shoreline but above it, backing the 25ft raised beach which is so evident along the Sound of Mull and the south side of Loch na Keal. They were a megalithic people who used crude implements of bone, stone and antlers. Such artifacts have been found at Quinish and Ulva Ferry.

There followed the Neolithic Age where a new type of burial procedure came to be observed, stone structures covered by earth to form a great mound. There was also an improvement in tools, and a first appearance of crude pottery – items were discovered at Mingary, Quinish, and elsewhere in the north of Mull, and at Uisken in the Ross of Mull, and in Iona. These people were the first true settlers in Mull.

The building of chambered cairns and mounds was to continue over the next thousand years, most of them being oval or circular structures of upright blocks of stone, roofed over by one or more massive slabs, all covered over. Rudimentary farming was developing, and by the time the Neolithic had merged into the Bronze Age in about 2500BC there had been a steady improvement in implements, also the introduction of metals as well as a distinctive type of pottery known as 'beaker ware'.

This was the age for the building of ritual monuments, of which so many have survived: burial cairns and cists, standing stones, stone circles, and cup and ring markings – the last-named are rare in Mull, but notably there are two cup-marked boulders in the 'Druids' Field' on top of the low cliff south-west of Calgary Bay, the cup-shaped hollows being about 2in (5cm) in diameter. The many sites may be seen as a reminder of Mull's participation in a widespread culture that encompassed almost the whole of Ireland and the western coasts of England, Wales, Scotland and the islands at a period well over a thousand years BC.

This dominant race must have been resident at the time of the Celtic invasion of south-west Scotland, invaders who later established the king-

Standing stones in the woods above Dervaig

Left: Standing stone at Lochbuie

dom of Dalriada. We marvel at the accuracy with which they set up and aligned standing stones and stone circles with distant objects so that certain combinations of shadows, and particular heavenly bodies would be in evidence at exact dates, thus providing a 'calendar' for the observance of religious rites, festivals, sowing, planting and so on. Many of the stones have disappeared, covered by accumulated soil or peat, used as gate posts, or even been integrated into a wall as at Kilmore cemetery at Dervaig, where in construction of the new part, one block of stone saved the handling of a ton of ordinary building stones.

The Bronze Age overlapped with the Iron Age between about 600BC to AD400 and more archaeological evidence exists in the survival of *crannogs*, or lake dwellings, of which at least six have been identified in Mull, in various localities. One such structure was uncovered in Loch na Mial, two miles south of Tobermory, when the loch was partly drained in the mid nineteenth century; moreover as a bonus, two dug-out canoes were found preserved in the mud. *Crannogs* were in fact artificial islands situated off the shores of lochs; some were just an accumulation of piles of stones, logs and brush-wood built up underwater and topped with a structure on which a habitation could be set up. They were usually connected with the shore by a zig-zag causeway of stepping stones designed to mislead intruders.

THE COMING OF THE CELTS

SUCH WERE the social conditions that ushered in the Iron Age, when the island had become an attractive place in which to settle, with good soil, timber and wildlife – favourable conditions which attracted unwelcome newcomers. It was doubly unfortunate that in Europe this was a time of expanding population, with pressure on living space, and when weapons and implements of iron were making both agriculture and methods of aggression easier. It is at this time that the Celts enter massively into the local scene. (May we, at this point comment on the pronunciation of the word 'Celt', or 'Celtic'? In some quarters there is a tendency to harden the 'C' to 'K', making 'Kelt' or 'Keltic'. Ignoring the fact that a 'kelt' is a spent salmon, the hardening of this lovely, soft word is also deprecated by such an authority on the pronunciation of English as H. W. Fowler.)

T. G. E. Powell, in Stuart Piggott's *The Prehistoric Peoples of Scotland*, reminds us that the Celts were a transalpine people known to Greek and Latin classical writers as early as the sixth century BC; powerful, warlike and restless, they became involved in the outward migrations and reached Britain as invaders, bringing a new Iron Age culture. They spread north to Scotland, and so Mull suffered its first great hostile invasion. It can be speculated, however, that the megalithic monuments probably continued to be used for their ritual purposes, and even provided something of a unifying force among invaders and invaded.

The first colonies of Celtic-Irish-Scots were probably settled in Mull by the early part of the second century AD; by the fifth century the island was part of the Scots kingdom of Dalriada, which extended from Wester Ross to south Argyll.

Now, Mull was not colonised without stout opposition by the earlier settlers against the successive waves of incomers. It was in this period that about forty duns and forts were constructed that can still be identified, chiefly around the west and south coasts of the island, facing the sea-borne invaders. They were built on the summits of low hills, or on the ends of coastal or inland promontories, on low knolls or rocky crags. Most of them were designed for short-time defence. Dun Aisgean is one fine example which can be seen – and easily reached – about half a mile south-south-west of Burg farmhouse at Torloisk. Measuring 34ft (10.4m) within its circular wall, which is well preserved, it sits on top of a rocky knoll on the 100ft pre-glacial raised beach; an area of good, though bracken-infested land lies beside it. It is surrounded by an outer defensive wall standing at the edge of the knoll outside the structures.

There were also defences known as vitrified forts, probably created by burning massive timbers within the rocky materials constituting the walls, which effectively melted and solidified the adjoining rocks. One such fort may be Dun Urgabul, a few hundred yards north of the road to Glengorm, about two miles from Tobermory.

Highland cow and calf near Gribun

THE VIKING INVASION

INTO THIS SETTLED ISLAND, populated now by the dominant Celtic-Scots, two new events were to intrude, one beneficial, the other menacing. Christianity, introduced by St Columba in the year 563, was to benefit the people generally, and in particular it made Iona a centre from which it was to spread far across Scotland, and beyond. The menace was the arrival of the Vikings. In about the year 800 certain events in Norway led to a movement of its people westwards; the Norsemen were warlike and adapted to the sea rather than to the land, and the independent Scottish tribes could not present a united front to the sea-raiders. It was a time when duns and forts in Mull were once again brought into use against the roving pirates.

In the Western Isles, Norse colonisation was dominant from the eighth to the thirteenth century, and Mull shared this very formative period of cultural history. The derivation of place-names in the Western Isles reflects the influence of the Norsemen: for example in the 'Long Island', Lewis to Barra, more permanent winter quarters were established and Norse elements in the place-names predominate in the ratio of four Norse to one Gaelic; in Mull the ratio is 1:1, with the Norse influence more apparent in the west and south coasts. Gaelic names predominate inland, however, for the roving sea-raiders generally confined themselves to the coasts where the configurations served as navigational aids.

As time went on and raiding on Iona ceased, Christianity was accepted by the Norsemen so effectively that towards the end of their domination responsibility for the administration of the affairs of Iona was shared with Trondheim in Norway. However, the power of the Vikings was largely ended by the decisive battle of Largs, in north Ayrshire when the fleet and invading force of King Haco were beaten; and in the northern Hebrides, the remaining power of the Norsemen was ended by Somerled, the great fighting progenitor of the Clan Donald, and in time to hold the title of Lord of the Isles.

CLANS AND CASTLES

WITH THE ENDING of Viking dominance a new social order emerged: the old order of leadership through the female line was replaced by the male; and the former 'mormaers' were replaced by the chiefs of the emerging clans. A clan is defined as 'a social group or an aggregate of distinct families actually descended from a common ancestor, and received by the King, through the Lord Lyon King of Arms, as an honourable community'. The clan system has been called 'the finest example of benevolent feudalism in Europe'. Note that the clan chiefs owed their allegiance not to parliament, but direct to the king, which led to much of the unrest among Highland clans when the royal line of kings deviated from what was hailed to be the correct and traditional line – Celtic to Norman, Cromwell, Stewart to Hanovarian.

The clan system was most effective in the fifteenth and sixteenth centuries, but from then on it began to break up under increasing pressure from the Scottish parliament. Following the union of the parliaments and the Jacobite uprisings, the British Government systematically destroyed what was left of it.

Within the social hierarchy of a clan the chief held the clan territories in trust for his clansmen, with power to dispose of or award land for good services or otherwise. He himself was not necessarily a man of means, but his clan was proud to maintain him in a manner worthy of his leadership. He was adviser, judge and protector, and military leader in times of armed conflict. A man would be proud to give his life to save his chief. As an example, in the year 1651 was the battle of Inverkeithing: fighting in support of King Charles II, Red Hector, 18th chief of the Macleans of Duart, with 800 of his own clansmen and 700 Buchanans, withstood for four hours the attacks of Cromwell's finest troops. In the heat of the battle Sir Hector was defended by seven brothers, all of whom were killed in turn warding off the attackers, each time another brother taking the place of the one that had fallen, and each as he fell called 'Another for Hector!' – and his successor as he stepped forward called defiantly 'Death for Hector!' That was the type of devotion displayed by a clansman to his chief. Only forty Macleans survived the battle, and since that time 'Another for Hector' has been a motto and watchword whenever a Maclean faces sudden danger.

TYPICAL DIET

Their chief diet was potatoes, introduced in the sixteenth century and which had become the staple diet by the nineteenth century. Other crops were kale, a coarse type of cabbage, and poor quality oats and barley. Before landlordism established a veto there was plenty of food such as venison, some meat from cattle and sheep, fish and sea-birds; for example the guga, the young of the puffin, were greatly esteemed, and were salted away in barrels for winter use.

Kinship was the feature of Gaelic society that survived the breakdown of the system itself, as witnessed by the response of clansmen in later years to follow their chiefs into arms, in spite of the fact that, after the mid-eighteenth century, those remaining were now simply lairds or landlords, often impoverished, or becoming so in their efforts to maintain their former pride and dignity among Society in the Lowlands.

In the larger clans a chief lived and travelled like a minor king. He had his 'seannachaidh', the 'wise man' and storyteller whose knowledge was invested in a prodigious memory; for there were few records kept except the title deeds to land which were often inscribed on sheepskins. From this arose the contemptuous reference by jealous or outwitted clans to 'The Campbells and their sheepskins', for that grasping clan ensured that any land they could claim was recorded on legal documents.

Such a chief had his private harper and piper, and his attendants, and even a 'wet-foot' who would carry him across streams in the absence of a pony so he remained 'dryshod'. He had his *birlinn* or galley if it was a maritime clan, and it is interesting to note that while the Viking galley was the prototype of the Highland galley, it was the Hebrideans who invented the rudder in place of the steering oar ('steerboard' which became 'starboard', the side on which the oar was mounted). Of course there was always the armed bodyguard, too, and the truth of the matter is that the traditional hospitality extended to this crowd when travelling was often a sore drain on many a family home.

There was no poverty, and the chief saw to it that the widows, the old and the infirm were cared for; destitution arose only when clans were broken up and left leaderless. Of course there were always the 'broken clans', people rejected from or expelled by other clans, for criminals were not tolerated within a clan. Grimly enough, losses in manpower through the regular military and inter-clan feuding kept the population at a level which the pastoral economy could support.

The people were housed in simple dwellings, with walls made of earth laced with timber or wattles; as time went on there was an increasing use of stone, usually a double wall built on the dry-stone principle and infilled with peat fragments or rubble, with smooth outer walls and rounded corners, surrounded by a causeway of flat stones. The tiny hamlets of Crakaig and Glacgugairidh in Treshnish (which we visit later) are excellent examples, that were still in use in the early nineteenth century. Chimneys were added towards the eighteenth century; before that the fire was kept burning in the centre of the floor, some of the smoke escaping through an opening in the roof above, which was of poles or timbers covered with turf or thatch of straw or heather. The room was therefore permanently filled with peat smoke just at head level, and this accounts for the low-set design of early furnishings.

Once a land of forests, by 1773 when the island was visited by Dr Johnson and Boswell, timber was so scarce that when people moved to

A representation of the lymphad (gael. long fhada) or galley of the Hebridean and maritime clans was rendered in simple terms for heraldic purposes, on coats of arms (here of the Clan Maclean) or shields and tombstones of the island chiefs

another house they took the roof off the one they were leaving and carried the timbers to roof their new habitation. Dwellings consisted of two sections, one for the occupants, the other for wintering their cattle, and the floor sloped gently down to the latter section. The presence of the cattle helped to keep the place warmer in winter. Cattle at that time were a smaller edition of the farouche-looking but gentle Highland we know today, and constituted the basic economy and money-earner of the community. Mull exported 5,000 animals annually to Oban and the markets of the south, including cattle from the islands and Ardnamurchan; these were landed in Mull at Croig in the north, Salen on the Sound of Mull, and Kintra in the Ross.

Despite the adverse descriptions offered by the occasional traveller such as 'insanitary hovels', these habitations were in fact far healthier than the overcrowded, filthy, disease-ridden slums of cities in the south at the time, even the Royal Mile in Edinburgh, from which plagues and epidemics were carried periodically to the Highlands and Islands. At least outside the homes of the people in the north were the rain and cleansing sea winds.

The names of the different clans arose from the name, peculiarity, or occupation of the progenitor – 'Mac', of course, simply means son, or descendant of this personality. For instance, Maclean is Mac-Gillean, 'Gillean' being the original head of the clan unit. An old Gaelic saying describes two of the most common Christian names; translated it says: 'As dogs lapping soup the names of the Macleans – Eachann-Lachann, Eachann-Lachann!' Similarly 'MacDonald' means 'sons of Donald'. Two names are interesting, referring to personal characteristics: Cameron is 'Twisted Nose' (Cam Sron); and Campbell, 'Twisted Mouth' (Cam Beul). Then there is Macintyre (Mac-an-t'Saoir'), 'Son of the Carpenter' – according to legend he inserted his thumb into a leak in the galley and cut it off, thus gaining recognition. Macnab (Mac-an-Aba) means the 'Son of the Abbot', the Lay Abbot of the monastery of St Fillan in Glendochart, Perthshire.

Mary MacDonald monument

CASTLES

THE ESTABLISHING OF THE CLAN SYSTEM led to the building of stout castles throughout the Highlands and Islands. The first influential clan in Mull was the Clan MacDougall of Lorn: centred in the Oban area, with their ruined castle of Dunollie overlooking Oban Bay, they built Duart Castle and Aros Castle during the thirteenth century (or the oldest portions of them at least). Because of their opposition to King Robert I, however, their possessions in Mull passed to the MacDonalds of Islay early in the fourteenth century. Adopting the title of Lord of the Isles (held today by our Prince Charles), and by marriage that of the Earls of Ross, the MacDonalds were the most powerful clan in the southern Hebrides. Traditional MacDonald histories confirm that Aros was a principal seat of the family during the fifteenth century.

Then in turn the 4th Lord of the Isles, John of Islay, was disciplined by an exasperated Scottish parliament towards the end of the sixteenth century, and the lands of Aros in Mull, with the castles of Duart and Aros, came into the hands of the Macleans on condition that they behaved themselves. In 1608 an expedition set out under Lord Ochiltree to bring the unruly island chiefs under control; many were invited on board one of the ships but under false pretences and were imprisoned; but then they were restored to freedom on promising to keep the peace.

In about 1674, after much disputing and finally bloodshed, the lands and castles of Duart and Aros – all the possessions of the Clan Maclean in Mull – passed into the hands of the Campbell Earls of Argyll; they were retained by them until various portions were sold to incoming lairds, leaving now just the south-west corner of the Ross of Mull as a foothold. The Campbells alleged that the Macleans were heavily indebted to them when they were forced to part with the island. In the same way MacQuarrie of Ulva, whose clan had held the island for 800 years, was obliged to sell it at the end of the eighteenth century to meet his indebtedness, although the Campbells were not involved.

DUART CASTLE

The name means 'Dark Headland', which is highly descriptive since the castle stands in a commanding position on the first point of the island passed on the way from Oban through the Sound of Mull. The two flats are entered from the great quadrangle, and inside there are a hundred apartments. When the MacDougalls fell from grace in the early fourteenth century, their possessions in Mull were conferred on the Lords of the Isles. Later, the custody of Duart was passed to Lachlan Maclean when he married Mary, daughter of John of Islay. When in turn the Lord of the Isles was punished by the Scottish parliament, the lands in Mull were transferred in 1476 to the Macleans, who then became the most powerful clan in the southern Hebrides.

However, difficult times were to follow for the Macleans: weakened by their military support of the Royalists, they were overrun first by Cromwell's forces, then by the Campbells – to whom, it was alleged, a considerable debt was owed by the Macleans. This was about 1692; from then on the castle was used for nothing more than as a barracks, until it fell into disrepair. Two centuries passed; then in 1911, Sir Fitzroy Donald Maclean, 10th Baronet of Duart and chief of the clan, with a distinguished army record, purchased Duart Castle, with 400 acres (160ha) of adjoining land, from Murray Guthrie of Torosay. The castle was restored, and re-occupied as the home of the chief. It is open to the public during the season and is a fascinating place to visit, with its numerous artifacts and relics.

An interesting report appeared in the *Herald* newspaper in April, 1994. It described how in 1979 a naval diver, searching the sea-bed for lobsters off Duart Point, came across cannons and artifacts around an old wreck. Later,

two similar wrecks were located nearby. Unaware of the importance of his find, the diver did not report it until 1991, when he led a diving team from the Historic Wrecks Association to the site. Here they identified one of the most significant and sensational finds ever discovered around the Scottish coasts. They are the wrecks of three English Warships of the seventeenth century, still, with their artifacts, in a good state of preservation.

Left: Duart Castle: clan centre and home of the chief of the Clan Maclean

In 1653 Cromwell, at the peak of his power, sent a fleet of six warships, with soldiers, to discipline the rebellious Macleans, who took successful elusive action. A sudden storm arose, catching the fleet unprepared and three of the vessels were sunk; *Swan*, *Martha & Margaret*, and *Speedwell*. Now under the control of the Historic Scottish Department, with marine archaeologist Dr Colin Martin, of St Andrews University, in charge, the wrecks are being preserved for systematic investigation over the next few years. Some of the finds are already on show in Duart Castle, a wonderful addition to the many interesting items on display.

AROS CASTLE

'Aros' is a Scandinavian word meaning 'an estuary', as in Aarhus, Denmark. The ruins stand commandingly at the edge of a bold bluff just north of Salen Bay, 8–9 miles from Tobermory and a few hundred yards from good arable ground, the main road and the little salmon river. Reduced now to a few crumbling walls and masses of rubble, it was a substantial hall-house and bailey with defences on the flat landward side, where the ruins of a small chapel can also be seen. Like Duart, Aros Castle was built by the MacDougalls in the thirteenth century; the design of the walls is the same, built to a thickness of 10ft (3m) or more, and depending on massiveness rather than on skill in the building. Like Duart, it too was one of the main establishments of the Lords of the Isles, and suffered the same sequence of ownership as Duart. There is an old tradition that the treasure of the Spanish galleon sunk in Tobermory Bay in 1588 was recovered by the Macleans and still lies hidden deep under the ruins of Aros Castle.

Aros Castle and a ruined cottage

Previous page: Moy Castle

MOY CASTLE

This is the third of Mull's traditionally built castles. Standing above the shoreline beside a small stream at the head of Loch Buie, this castle is considered to have been built in the early fifteenth century by Hector Maclean, brother of Lachlan Maclean of Duart and the progenitor of the renamed Maclaines of Lochbuie, who made it their home. It had three storeys and a garret, and is more of a tower house than a defensive centre like Duart and Aros. At floor level (which is solid rock) there is a small well of good water which refills as fast as it is emptied, with no overflow. A small pit prison, known as a bottle dungeon, was built into the stonework of the wall, with access from the first floor.

Confiscated, like Duart and Aros, during the Civil War, and garrisoned by Campbell followers, the castle was later restored to the Macleans; however it was abandoned as a residence in 1752 when a new house was built – this was described in rather disparaging terms by Boswell during his visit in 1773. Although roofless, the castle is still impressive to view from the outside, but because of the risk of danger from crumbling masonry the entrance door is barred.

DUNARA

Less accessible and not as impressive as the three principal castles, the ruins of Dunara stand on the summit of one of the flat little plateaux near Sorne Point, Glengorm, with a convenient inlet for boat landings. It probably stands on the site of a much older structure. It seems to have consisted of several buildings of a more domestic nature, the main defence being a curtain wall of stone and lime enclosing the entire area of the flat summit. This castle was probably the main stronghold of the Clan MacKinnon which held the surrounding lands of Mishnish as early as 1354. In the seventeenth century the Macleans took over the lands of Mishnish and the MacKinnons concentrated on their main clan lands in Skye.

DUN BAN

Again, like Dunara, this is in an excellent defensive position. It is known as Glackindaline Castle, or Dun Ban, and lies on a small rocky tidal island between the islands of Ulva and Gometra, with a good landing place. Although built in late medieval times, it was a secure home for the MacQuarrie chiefs of Ulva until a more comfortable residence was built in more settled times. A portion of the walls of this later home is still standing at the estate office near the present Ulva House at the east end of the island. This old house is where Dr Johnson and Boswell were entertained by the MacQuarrie chief during their tour.

CAIRNBURG MOR AND CAIRNBURG BEAG

Finally there is the unusual 'castle' of Cairnburg Mor and its supporting defences on the adjoining island of Cairnburg Beag, the northernmost of the Treshnish Islands that lie about three miles to the north-west of Mull. They are impregnable fortress-islands – at least Cairnburg Mor certainly is, being strategically situated to command the sea-lanes to the Inner Hebrides, but with neither a safe anchorage nor a dependable landing place on the strip of rocky shore on account of the stormy seas and tides that run like rivers between the reefs and islands. Their history goes back to 1249, for in that year, according to the statement in *Pennant's Tour* of 1772, John Dungadi was appointed by Acho, king of the Nordeneys (the northern sphere of Norse territorial claims in the Hebrides), to defend the two islands. He held out for a long time under pressure, even after the Norse rulers had been expelled. After the Treaty of Perth in 1266 it was regarded as a royal castle, a possession of the MacDougalls; however, they lost the custody of it in 1343 to the Lord of the Isles; later, like Duart and Aros, it passed to the Macleans, and finally, in 1692, it fell into the hands of the Campbells.

It is formed by a flat summit of a sea-girt plateau, dropping in 120ft (37m) cliffs into the sea on three sides and to a narrow, rocky beach on the north-east side; its defences consisted of walling along the edges of the cliffs instead of massive buildings. Light cannon could fire from built-in emplacements through embrasures in the walls. Only one very steep path was left to give access to the top through an entrance gateway, but it was a death-trap for attackers since boulders could be rolled down it from a stockpile above. Defenders were accommodated in a narrow gully which was roofed with timbers and turfed over. There is the ruin of a thick-walled, two-roomed house that was used as a refuge or a prison as the case might be. There are also the ruins of a small chapel nearby.

Fresh water was obtained from rainwater dammed back to form a small pond, which would have had to have been protected from fouling by the colonies of sea-birds. On the shore there is also a tiny rock basin called the 'Well of the Half Gallon' which refills with good water as fast as it is emptied.

Cairnburg Beag follows the same pattern of defensive measures but on a much lower and less ambitious scale, partly on the foreshore, and partly on the elevated eastern portion; it seems to be more a back-up to the main defences of its larger neighbour.

4 MULL AND THE CLEARANCES

TRAVELLING THROUGH MULL, the visitor cannot fail to notice the great number of pathetic little rectangles of ruined walls: these were once homes, built by a contented peasantry wishing for nothing more than to be left alone to enjoy its traditional livelihood and way of life. The ruins are memorials to a hundred years of greed, arrogance and inhumanity on the part of a new race of landowners and a distant, indifferent government.

The story of the Clearances of the late eighteenth and nineteenth centuries is well known. However, for the benefit of those not fully acquainted with the subject, we shall give a short summary of the sequence of events, with extracts from the official records of evidence given before the Land Courts which describe some details of the actions of landlords in Mull. Without such records some of those actions could well be dismissed as incredible.

There were three classes of tenant: first, the tacksman (a 'tack' was a form of lease) who held land with a rented value of £50 or more, and dealt direct with the landowner; they were families of influence, with a good social background. Then there were the crofters, with, or sometimes without a formal lease, whose rental did not exceed £20. Finally there were the cottars, by far the greatest number, whose holdings were let according to the traditional rights-by-use-and-wont of the ordinary clansfolk. They had no official title or lease, and paid a rent to the landowner – formerly the chief – in services in addition to hard cash, which for them was a scarce commodity. They depended entirely on a cattle economy, for which the use of open grazing was essential.

The Battle of Culloden in 1746 was followed by harsh punitive measures and laws which effectively destroyed the clan system and ended the power and social presence of the chiefs. Rebellious chiefs were seized and executed, or fled abroad, leaving their clan lands leaderless. The rich grazings in now ownerless districts aroused the interest of agricultural profiteers who proposed substituting the more profitable Cheviot sheep for the traditional black cattle. Wealthy landowners in the south began to buy or rent estates, but to be run as sheep farms.

Arrogance and a certain contempt by the 'upper classes' for the 'lower classes' led to callous, unopposed 'clearances', that is, the eviction of tenants so that their lands could be turned over to sheep – and no mention of

Left: The old school house at Gribun; now a holiday cottage

compensation. As if such conditions were not enough, the British Isles, and particularly Ireland and the mild western seaboard of Scotland, were smitten by two years of potato disease that practically wiped out what had become the staple diet of the people. *Phytophthora Infestens* was a fungal, wind-blown disease that originated in Belgium in early 1845, spreading rapidly and reaching its peak in Scotland in 1846. At first the government, acting under Robert Peel who was soon to retire, assisted with oatmeal and imports of maize from North America; but that was soon discontinued when the Clergy incredibly made the hypocritical submission that the calamity was an act of God, had to be endured, and should not be interfered with by famine relief! Conditions in Ireland were even worse than in Scotland, leading to starvation, deaths and the emigration of two million people between 1845 and 1851.

People were left destitute, and there was nothing they could do except move to uncongenial industrial jobs in the south, emigrate, or fall back as paupers on parish relief and church donations; alternatively they could work on roads, drainage, walls and so on, but for a pittance – subsistence 'wages' paid in oatmeal and other victuals from small government grants. Furthermore these were administered by the landowners and too often diverted for their own private use – and even used as fodder for livestock. Gifts of food were sometimes received from more fortunate friends overseas. In all 20,000 people had emigrated from the Highlands and Islands by 1800.

Pauperism led to the building of poorhouses by parish councils between 1850 and 1870, but there was never any government intervention, except for the small subsistence grants.

Then in the late 1870s public interest at last became aroused. Press publicity followed, questions were raised by influential people and the government was forced into belated action. The Napier Commission was formed in 1883, followed by the setting up of Land Courts, to enquire into the question. During the sitting of the Courts, no fewer than 46,450 questions were raised by 6,000 objecting witnesses throughout the Highlands and Islands; these were recorded in thirty volumes that can be consulted by arrangement in any library. Immediate action followed and oppressive rents were slashed; but by that time no court could possibly meet the demands of the objectors for a restoration of lost lands and compensation.

However, as a result of this action, a new deal was created for the crofters. A permanent Crofters' Commission was appointed which operates to the present day; and crofters – no longer cottars – were confirmed in their holdings at controlled rents, with various amending Acts allowing holdings to be passed on to their families, or even to be sold.

In the meantime, imports of sheep products from the developing colonies were coming in to undercut prices in the home markets, and sheep farming was no longer profitable. Further, in too many districts overgrazing had fouled the land, making it no longer fit for cattle even if the substitution had been considered, and the grazings reverted to bog, bracken and heather. Much of this was useless for any purpose other than being added to sporting estates, which already covered so much of the Highlands.

A new order began in the Highlands facilitated by better communications, and improving designs of sporting guns and rifles: Sporting estates became fashionable among the wealthy, and there appeared a new 'Balmorality', as one cynic called it – a fashionable, imitative policy whereby incongruous mansions and shooting lodges were built in unspoilt Highland glens, following the example of Queen Victoria at Balmoral, on Deeside. Sir Walter Scott's earlier writings had glamorised the Highlands and the Highlander, and laid the foundations of a tourist industry that was to escalate to the vital part it plays in the Scottish economy today. The Queen's apparent love for the Highlands expressed in her writings, her tours, and the presence of railways and steamboats brought more and more people to explore the Highlands. But it is a mystery how Queen Victoria failed to be aware of the exploitation of her subjects here; an expression of her displeasure could have gone a long way towards redressing the evil.

But let us be fair. Those sporting estates helped to hold together the dwindling population, small oases of limited prosperity. There were real improvements through the creation of larger and more economic farms, introducing modern methods, new crops, better breeds of livestock – but unfortunately, fewer workers. Deciduous woodlands and shelter belts began to feature in an otherwise bare landscape; and many of them are still growing today as valuable timber. There was a slow dwindling of the former arrogance which was replaced by a mutual respect, by the lairds for the skill of their staffs, and by the staffs for the security and better conditions now offered. Employment was steady, housing improved, and village communities were often kept alive through the upkeep of local estates, besides benefiting from the high taxes paid by the estates. But the clans were gone, and an historic way of life. The end of an old song.

CLEARANCES ON THE MULL ESTATES

IN THE YEAR 1818, writing about Mull, John Johnstone of Coll said:

> . . . a slow ruthless policy of evictions. All the lairds were in it with few exceptions. Poor people were compelled to work on roads, drains, walls, fences and piers for a scanty allowance of oatmeal and other victuals, much of it sent gratis from America to be distributed among the poor, just to keep them alive. This was exploited by the lairds to their advantage.

There were about twelve estates large and small during much of the period in Mull, but we have been able to find only one favourable report: that was MacDonald of Gribun, who did what he could to provide work and shelter for evicted people from elsewhere, whom he described as 'industrious and respectable'.

There follows now a condensed description of the various estates and the actions of the chief landowners, extracted from the evidence of reputable Mull witnesses as recorded in the Books of the Courts.

TOBERMORY ESTATE

This presented a challenge to successive lairds of the Aros estate in their desires for alleged 'improvements', a euphonious word for land-grabbing. In 1789 the Society for Extending the Fisheries and Improvements around the United Kingdom (hereafter referred to as 'The Society') selected a number of sites along the islands and the west coast as potential fishing centres, of which Tobermory was one. The estate was purchased from Hugh Maclean of Coll, who owned much of the north of Mull, and by 1800 a settlement was established with a population of 300. By 1808, 136 vessels were using the port; but high hopes for a successful herring industry were dashed when the unpredictable fish moved away from the area. However Tobermory became a busy centre for the district, having the finest bay and anchorage in the Hebrides.

Legal titles were given for the building of houses with gardens, and these were granted with 99-year leases, the holders to have rights to hill pasturages by arrangement with the Society's agent. Further, every inhabitant had the right to cut peats and extract stone for building. By 1840 there were 120 crofts around the village. Now, two of those concessions led to trouble in the future: the first was that there were no written entitlements for grazing rights; the second was that hill grazings could be excluded from the concession and returned to any new laird if 'improvements' were introduced.

This indeed happened in 1842 when David Nairne purchased part of Aros estate, where many of the crofts were situated. At once the new laird demanded much higher rents ('The higher the rent the better the work'), a subtle method of dealing with crofters who could not be evicted and which forced a number of them to give up their crofts, furthermore with no compensation offered for reclamation work they had carried out. Nairne then tried to take over part of the hill grazings, but as this formed part of the crofters' 'tack', or lease, they refused to comply. He proceeded to build a turf dyke to isolate the disputed area, calling it an 'improvement', but in this instance the settlers were able to bring their case before the House of Lords and were upheld in their objection. Not to be beaten, Nairne appealed to the Court of Session, which unaccountably decided in his favour, submitting that a turf dyke *was* an improvement (and so the grazing rights reverted to Nairne). Anticipation of further heavy legal costs prevented the settlers from renewing their case. This was a well-known tactic by landlords: to overcome opposition by appealing to the courts, knowing that the legal costs incurred in opposing them would be beyond the financial means of the objectors.

Nairne also carried out a number of evictions where the holders had no legal rights and he was unopposed.

Subsequent lairds of Aros followed the same sort of procedure, demanding the hill ground, then draining Loch na Mial to discourage stock from frequenting that part, submitting there were no legal titles, and also being rebuffed at law, for the settlers were now receiving the backing of the community. However, the repeated claims of the estate, right down to the laird Alexander Allan (who at least did something to improve the amenities of the village) so wore down the crofters that in spite of all their defending actions they finished up confined to just a few poor grazings, and even the digging of peat moved to inferior stretches of the moorland.

The typically spiteful attitude of the laird is revealed in the case of tenant Donald Colquhoun and another, who were stronger objectors. For their temerity they were blacklisted, and their names circulated among other estates in Mull as being 'undesirable tenants', to be refused any requests.

TOBERMORY AND THE ERRAY ESTATE

This estate lies north of Tobermory. Twenty crofts and hill grazings unwanted by the Society were transferred to the Erray estate, but on the north coast away from the influence of the Society, nine tenants were evicted at Reraig and eight at Ardmore. Erray became an exclusive zone, letting being granted only to private friends. Tobermory people were banned from the estate; even the popular path to the lighthouse was closed. The people found themselves hemmed in between Aros and Erray estates.

GLENGORM AND QUINISH

These are now separate estates. The picturesque little village of Dervaig ('the Little Grove') lies in the Quinish estate, built by Maclean of Coll, who had ambitions of setting up a small settlement at the head of Loch Cumhain, centred on Dervaig, where there is some good land. In about the year 1800 he sponsored the building of the one main street, over two dozen houses built in pairs with large gardens at the back; they all had hill grazings, too. Nearly all the old cottages in Dervaig have been altered or modernised, but one or two still show the original design.

Then in 1847 James Forsyth became the laird of Quinish and Glengorm (originally known as Sorne) and this wealthy stranger proved to be one of the most cunning and greedy of the new Mull lairds. The story of Dervaig's troubles is best told by referring to the evidence presented before the 1883 Commission held at Tobermory by Lachlan Kennedy, a well-respected Dervaig crofter.

A DEVOTED SON

On the Glengorm estate, near the shore, there was a small plot of land coveted by the laird. The land belonged to a woman who held legal title granted by a previous laird. Although she lived alone, grew few crops and had no obvious means of support, she lived comfortably and was able to pay the increasingly extortionate rent imposed by the laird in a vain effort to force her to give up. Few local people were aware that she had a devoted son who roved about the islands in a fast skiff. He followed some questionable practices such as sheep and cattle lifting, and running the occasional cargo of illicit spirits. Periodically, on dark nights, he came in to the Glengorm shore to visit his mother and give her more than enough cash and goods to keep her in comfort. This arrangement ended only with her death.

Dervaig; note the round steeple of Kilmore church

As usual, the laird's first target was rents: Kennedy reported that his was increased during the year, with further increases to follow. There were twenty-seven crofters in Dervaig with common grazings on Monabeg and Torr. Forsyth intimated he was prepared to take over those grazings for improvements, and return them in a much superior condition to the crofters after three years. They took Forsyth's word for this, and nothing was committed to writing. At the end of the three years he announced that he would return the grazings – which had been reduced in size because a proportion had been ploughed up for estate cropping – only on payment of what was an exorbitant rent, with a short lease and an annual payment to be made for fertilisers.

Of course the incensed crofters refused this imposition in a body, and at once Forsyth told them that he was withdrawing all rights to the grazings, without compensation, and no reduction in rents. He also told them he was taking over their livestock at his own valuation; any remaining unsold they could simply destroy. The crofters were thus forced to submit. The twenty-seven were reduced to thirteen, struggling to make a living; the others left the district.

John Campbell was another reliable witness who testified. He described how those people with a house and garden and also those all-important rights to hill grazings were cheated by Forsyth. Forsyth offered to give the people new titles and to carry out improvements if they would just sign new agreements. They were nearly all Gaelic speakers, knowing little English and even less about legal documents, and they signed in good faith – only to discover that they had signed away their rights to everything except house and garden with no reduction in rent; in other words they had nothing left to live on but the produce of their gardens.

Forsyth then turned his attention to the tenants of Glengorm, an estate immediately to the east of Quinish. Here the peasantry were unprotected cottars, whose land was soon cleared of their offending presence. Forsyth wished to build a fine new mansion house on the estate – we know it today as Glengorm Castle – and three crofts had to be cleared to provide a site for the building and the private policies round about. Trying to find a suitable name for the building he suggested Dunara, but was advised that the old fortress of Dunara lay not too many miles distant, and there could be confusion. Finally he condescended to ask the advice of an old woman who lived on the estate. 'Call your fine new house "Glengorm",' she replied. The laird was charmed with the name, which means 'Blue Glen'. The cynical old woman was secretly delighted, for her intention was to commemorate the days when the glen was indeed blue with the smoke from burning homesteads.

THE ISLAND OF ULVA

Probably the most heartless and sweeping clearances of all took place in Ulva. The island is divided from the Torloisk shore by a ferry trip of a few hundred yards; it had belonged to the Clan MacQuarrie for many hundreds of years, but was sold in about 1800 to meet the indebtedness of the chief. One of the succeeding lairds was Francis W. Clark, who bought the island in the 1830s and supplied detailed information in 1837 for the *Statistical Account* of 1845. In glowing terms he described the fertility of Ulva, his successful experiments in the growing of wheat and beans, and the export of nearly 900 barrels of potatoes of excellent quality from his home farm. Even the quality of the kelp was praised, for there was a short resumption of the kelp industry at about that time.

In 1837 Ulva had a contented self-supporting population of 604, increasing to 859 by 1840, including a small corner of the adjacent mainland of Mull. By 1881 only 57 people were left, and these were obliged to camp in precarious holdings in a corner of the island near the ferry that came to be known as Desolation Point; they were not allowed to build proper houses or plant trees in case this indicated some permanence. Two witnesses (among others) in later years, Lachlan MacQuarrie and Alex Fletcher, described what took place in Ulva during the 1840s:

> Clark's first step was to evict seventy-three householders, first moving them to small alternative holdings, then out of those, leaving them altogether destitute. They were cottars, of course, with no legal rights and no defence. Any family that ventured to protest simply had the roof torn off or burned, even with the furnishings of the house.

A CURSE ON THE LAIRD

Another story was told by another old Glengorm woman, who died in 1917: when Forsyth was about to inspect his completed house and opened the front door, a bat flew out into his face. This, the people declared, was the soul of one particular cottar who had been evicted under unusually harsh conditions and had laid a curse on the laird to the effect that he would never sleep in his new house. Strangely enough, the laird did contract an illness immediately after this incident, and died before he could take up residence.

CLARK'S BURIAL

The dislike in which Clark was held is reflected in the following legend: that when he died and his coffin was delivered at the ferry, it could not be moved until a spell was invoked to release it from the powers of evil. He is buried in the tiny family burial place on top of the peculiar little hillock at the east end of the island.

Clark, when appealed to, simply rebuffed the applicants with the remark: 'No; I am not your father!' Even an old woman who was sick and bedridden, and living with her daughter, was not spared: off came the roof, except for a small portion above her bed as a temporary shelter.

A further misfortune came in the mid-1840s when for two years running the potato crop was all but lost because of disease that swept the Highlands, and especially the western islands – potatoes had become almost a staple diet.

The tales related of Francis Clark's inhumanity are legion. When I was a small boy, an old man said to me: 'when I was a little boy like you, I remember my father carrying me out of our cottage in Ulva, which had been built by our grandfather. We were hardly out of the door than the factor and his men waiting there pushed blazing torches into the thatch, and all that was left were the walls.'

Another old woman told us that when she had been evicted and was desperate, she appealed to Clark to give her just any kind of shelter at all; to which he replied 'No; but I'll tell you how I will help you. I am on the committee of the new poorhouses at Tobermory [built in 1862] and I shall see that you are admitted.'

This unbalanced laird even tore washing from the lines and filled in a well with his own hands by way of punishing people who were temporarily forced to live within sight of his house. Finally nothing was left but sheep and a handful of estate workers.

THE ARGYLL ESTATES

WE DELIBERATELY KEEP to the spelling 'Argyll', for in earlier times it was 'Argyle'.

In 1847 George Douglas Campbell, 8th Duke of Argyll and chief of the Clan Campbell, took over the Campbell lands in Mull. He is described as a cold, grasping, calculating man who was later called to question for his oppressive methods. He appointed Duncan Forbes to be his factor, but Forbes left after a month, disgusted with the tyranny of the exorbitant rents newly instigated by the duke. Other factors were admittedly inexperienced in the ways of the islanders, but any mistakes in increased rents appear to have been welcomed.

In 1849 Campbell evicted a large number of cottars at Kilfinichen on the north side of Loch Scridain. Twenty-six were able to emigrate to America; others were moved to Kinloch at the head of Loch Scridain where they lived in poverty, not being allowed to cultivate the land. Their livestock and certain effects had to be sold to meet high rents of between £5 and £15 per annum, which reduced some of the people to abject pauperism.

In Bunessan, 243 adults and children were assisted to emigrate by a grant from the Relief Fund. This was when glowing reports were publicised

The effigy of George Dougald Campbell, 8th Duke of Argyll, 1823 – 1900. It is carved from a block of Carrara marble

on the benefits of emigrating to Canada or America where prosperity awaited them. How happy their relatives were overseas! All this propaganda was allowed to be disseminated unchecked by the government – a government that allowed the widespread exploitation of its people and their transportation in disease-ridden and often unseaworthy ships, landing emigrants in an inhospitable environment and abandoning them to cope with further hardships.

The Duke decreed that all rents were to be paid direct to him and not through factors, which gave him an even more direct rule over the tenants. Widows were not allowed to retain holdings. Loans were given to crofters to induce them to buy boats and gear and take up fishing, but were only granted if the tenants agreed to give up their holdings and exchange them for alternatives beside the shore, usually inferior and where the ground required breaking in. The project failed: the people were born agriculturalists; fishing was alien, they were inexperienced, and they were left much worse off in their indifferent new holdings.

In 1847 Campbell turned his attention to Iona, where the population in 1840 had been about 500. Here, rents were doubled and grazing confiscated and the cottars were compelled to give part-time service to the Duke. Holdings were cleared and amalgamated, and then let to friends of the Duke as good farms.

The foregoing are a few items from the evidence given by the two witnesses Duncan Maclean and Lachlan MacDonald of Ardalanish before the 1883 Commission. At Ardalanish, twelve families had been evicted to provide grazing for a sheep farm. The Duke's ambition was to set up larger, unobstructed farm units or sheep grazings – but at the expense of a whole people's livelihood and way of life. The first action of the Land Courts here, as elsewhere in Mull, was to reduce rents by 40 per cent.

LOCHBUIE, GLENBYRE AND CROGGAN

In the year 1894 the local paper the *Oban Times* reported as follows:

> In 1884 there were 91 households with 500 people employed in crofting and fishing, a comparatively prosperous community. By 1894 there remained 42 households and 250 people. Crofts had been taken over by Maclaine of Lochbuie and amalgamated into a deer forest. The countryside was dotted with ruins.

Within the area of Kinlochspelve and Lochbuie there were 10,000 acres including some of the finest grazings and arable land in Mull (the area known as the 'Garden of Mull'). Most of it was now a sporting estate with three shooting lodges and only a handful of gamekeeping staff.

Two witnesses before the Courts gave evidence that earlier, in 1861, there had been twenty-five people in the little hamlet of Kinloch. They were evicted by Maclaine in 1865, and fifteen crofts, along with the hill grazings, were amalgamated into two farms. In addition, all the rents had been raised. Old people were forced to live under shocking conditions that led to their deaths. This was on the south side of Loch Scridain where there was nothing but misery. The north side of the loch was fertile and productive, but there, too, a new laird, Mitchell, bought this portion in 1873 and systematically cleared the whole area. He suggested that the people could exist on fishing, regardless of the fact that no capital was provided for boats or gear, or – like crofters elsewhere in Mull – that their experience of fishing was nil.

TOROSAY ESTATE

This part of the Argyll estates was sold to Campbell of Possil. There were the usual evictions, although the most sweeping were carried out earlier in the nineteenth century in Glenforsa, a fertile glen populated from the earliest times. The glen extends from the Sound of Mull to Glen More near that shapely mountain, Ben Talla (Talaidh, 'Prospect Hill').

Torosay estate included the village of Salen, a small residential village with a pier whose site had to be changed twice on account of strong tidal currents and the introduction of deeper-draught ships. The estate was purchased in 1875 by Murray Guthrie; in 1911 he sold Duart Castle and the adjoining 400 acres to Sir Fitzroy Maclean, who restored the castle in 1912.

The first carriage road in Mull was built between Grass Point (the original ferry to Oban) and Salen by the dispossessed people of Mull. It was twenty miles in length, with five bridges.

Right: Torosay Castle. Magnificent nineteenth century mansion house connected with Craignure by the 1½ mile Mull railway

THE CANADIAN BOAT SONG

In the book The Highland Clearances *by Alex Mackenzie there is reference to that sad, well-known poem of the emigrants* The Canadian Boat Song. *The authorship of this poem has been in doubt, but Mackenzie's book quotes a poem written by the Rev Donald Macleod, DD, father of Lord Macleod of Fuinary and the famous sponsor to the Iona Community. It was published in* Good Words *for August 1882, when the author was moving from his charge in Fuinary (on the Morvern shore across the Sound of Mull from Tobermory) to a new charge on the mainland in the south. The verse from the minister's poem* Farewell to Fuinary *may well be the original, differing in only a few details from the modern version:*

> *From the dim shieling of the*
> *   misty island*
> *Mountains divide us and a*
> *   waste of seas.*
> *But still our hearts are true, our*
> *   hearts are Highland*
> *And in our dreams we behold*
> *   the Hebrides.*
> *Tall are those mountains and*
> *   the woods are grand*
> *But we are exiled from our*
> *   father's land.*

One annual event held on the Torosay estate still survives: nowadays as the Mull and Morvern Agricultural Show held at Aros Bridge annually in August. It began as a horse fair about two hundred years ago, held in Torosay parish every 21 August. There were once fine woodlands in the parish, but after the late eighteenth century they were mostly cut down to provide charcoal for the Lorne Furnace Company of Argyll, for the making of explosives.

TORLOISK ESTATE

This estate was owned by the Marquis of Northampton who was connected by marriage with the Macleans of Torloisk. Records here are not so detailed, except that thirty-two evictions were carried out to extend the private lands of the proprietor. Calgary, Treshnish and Caliach had their Clearances, and

POPULATION STATISTICS

Year	Population of whole island	Population of Tobermory
1789	-	200
1801	8,539	456
1811	9,383	550
1821	10,612	850
1851	8,369	1,540
1871	5,017	1,850
1891	3,463	1,265
1911	4,173	900
1921	3,754	850
1931	3,160	772
1951	2,693	693
1961	2,343	668
1969	2,100	610
1981	2,365	683

More attractive employment and education facilities in the south have kept the population of Mull static or falling during most of the twentieth century.

Looking west from Calgary Bay

at least one emigrant ship sailed from Calgary Bay. This may have been in about 1817 when the estate of Mornish came into the hands of Allan McAskill, together with the settlements of Arin and Inivea, above the north shore of Calgary Bay, which were also duly cleared. Inivea was a township of about two dozen houses built at the end of the eighteenth century, and some of the ruins are preserved to the wall-heads; like Crakaig and Glacgugairidh on the south of Treshnish estate, they are excellent examples of early stone houses.

The reader has been taken round Mull and seen enough evidence to reveal the widespread evils of the Clearances. The statistics at the end speak for themselves, even if there has been some confusion in dates and the change-over in estate ownerships, for the dates have not always been clearly brought out in the Court Records.

5 EXPLORING MULL

DEER STALKING

During the stalking season (mid-August to mid-October) it is wise to contact those in charge of an estate before setting out, to ensure that no stalking is to take place near the proposed route, because the sight of a strange figure can send the deer moving for miles and ruin an organised stalk. Estates are highly expensive to run and have an important place in the economy.

AT THE TIME OF WRITING there is some discussion about hill walking and rights of way, and it may be that newcomers to Mull or the Highlands would welcome a few suggestions about preserving the privileges of the public. Nevertheless we must always remember that even the largest Highland estate, however remote, is still as much private property as our own front garden. The great difference is that with a proper approach, neither harm nor intrusion is caused when we walk the hills or shores and climb the mountains. However, it is our duty, not only to the landowners but also to the environment, to keep the countryside tidy, to avoid damage to walls and fences and vegetation, and to keep dogs under strict control in the presence of livestock; and of course it is only courteous to avoid intruding on private buildings or surroundings.

In return for his consideration, an explorer should expect freedom and cooperation; there is no place for arrogance or an encroachment on rights of access, and even in Mull there have been a few hints along these lines:

Leave nothing but your footprints;
Take away nothing but what you brought in.

Whether by car or on foot you will find a country of endless variety to explore. There are no buses to take you around except along the main road between Craignure and Iona, and Craignure and Tobermory. Touring buses wait at Craignure to take people on tours around the island, giving a quick impression of what the visitor shall learn in detail – sometimes a lift may be had with Royal Mail transport. The enjoyment of the magnificent views, the artifacts, geological features, places or objects of historical or traditional interest really depend on travelling by car or in more leisurely fashion, on your own two feet. Drivers will find that Mull roads require a different standard of driving. On the single track roads there are plenty of passing places to allow for overtaking as well as for *being overtaken*: the man in your mirror may be a local person on business, or some harassed visitor late as usual for catching the ferry and thoroughly frustrated by your meandering progress. Beware of sheep on unfenced roads, especially early in the season when lambs are about; a sheep on one side of the road and her lamb on the other obviously present a potential problem.

Having issued all the necessary caveats, let us proceed to explore the island: it is probably more interesting to present Mull in three sections.

Left: Creag Mhór. A stretch of the dangerous road at the foot of the 100ft (303m) cliffs of Gribun

NORTHERN MULL

. . . the little roads where the roads go up and the mists come down.

WHETHER YOU LAND at Craignure or Fishnish (from Lochaline in Morvern) you are facing the main road: to the right for Salen (12 miles/19km) and Tobermory (22 miles/36km), to the left for Iona (30 miles/48km). We suggest you head first for the north of Mull with Tobermory as a starting point, for we feel it has more appeal and preserves more of the traditional atmosphere.

But before we start out at Craignure, leave the car at the pierhead and walk the few hundred yards round the bay to the railway station. Yes here is the start of Mull's passenger railway, although it is only of 10^{1}/4 in (26cm) gauge and 1^{1}/2 miles (2.4km) of track. It passes through the woods with glimpses of the far mountains towards Ben Nevis and Glencoe, lazy pheasants moving out of its way, to the terminus at Torosay Castle. This fine building was built by David Bryce in 1856; it has extensive terraced gardens in which you will find the ornamental statue walk designed by John Lorimer in 1899. The house contains many items of both family and general interest, and has a tea-room in which to relax before taking to the road.

The road follows the level coastline, dominated to the left by the long ridge of Dun da Ghaoithe (2,512ft/766m), Hill of the Two Winds, so called because at the summit the winds are deflected by the configuration. Crossing the bridge over the little salmon river the Forsa, we see the glen of that name extending to the south, blocked by the shapely 'sugar loaf' Ben

The Isle of Mull Railway. A private venture from Craignure to Torosay Castle

Talaidh, the Prospect Hill (2,498ft/758m). We pass Mull airfield beside the Log House Hotel, a grass runway of 3,000ft (915m) in length by 90ft (27m) in width.

Before we reach the village of Salen (population 260) you will notice the pre-Reformation ruined chapel of Pennygown, with its surrounding cemetery, beside the road. There are fourteen such chapels identified in Mull, and this is one of the best preserved. Look outside at the south-east corner of the building: where you will see two recumbent graveslabs, one of a woman, the other of a man in the panoply of a Highland fighting man. These are said to be the resting places of 'the only bad chief of Duart' and his wife, both of whom were so involved in witchcraft that they were refused interment within the holy ground of the chapel itself, although they were granted to lie as near to it as possible. A recognised feature of those old graveslabs is that if the armed figure has its legs crossed, it indicates he fought with the Crusades.

At the village of Salen a road strikes off to the west across the three-mile isthmus to the head of Loch na Keal, where it joins the west coast road we shall explore later. At Salen our fine road ends, and the remaining twelve miles to Tobermory are in such a condition as had been tolerated for decades by an exasperated population of Tobermory, for this is just as busy a road as the previous section. At the bridge which crosses the small salmon river the Aros, a side road bears left beside the river and continues for ten miles across Mull to Dervaig. Ruined Aros Castle, that we have already described, stands on its promontory above Aros bridge.

Admire the magnificent stretch of the Sound of Mull from the summit, the 'Black Slope', then pass through the woods of Aros estate and you will come to the crossroads at the bridge over the Tobermory river; turn sharp right down the steep hill, passing the distillery at the foot, and you will see the colourful main street in front of you. It is a real suntrap, curving round the north side of the finest bay in the Hebrides to MacBraynes' pier with the old pier in the centre, now piled with the gear of local fishermen. It is an excellent yachting centre with every facility, from stores to baths at the local hotels. The story of the Spanish galleon blown up and sunk in 1588 is well described in Alison McLay's book *The Tobermory Treasure*.

Just over a mile from Tobermory you will see a flat area surrounded by a wall – this marks the site of the former Mull Combination Poorhouse we have mentioned, with the Tobermory river bisecting the five-acre property; only the former lodge remains, now a modernised dwelling. After three miles we come to the three Mishnish lochs, where the big fat brown trout wait for the angler (permission to fish must be sought at Brown's, in Tobermory). Halfway along, just beside the lonely ruined Loch House, a wall runs up the hill: follow it, and it will take you to the top of the hill 'S Airde Ben (959ft/292m), one of the lesser volcanoes that broke through the earlier piled-up lavas. There is a deep little loch in the former crater. Although not one of the high hills, the views from this isolated height are superb.

TOBERMORY

We have already told you some of the early history of the place; the name means 'Well of Mary', although the site of the original well is uncertain, below what is now the cemetery. It would take up too much space to tell you what to see and do here; better to call at the Tourist Centre in Main Street for advice and literature on everything from golf to deep sea angling. It is a very busy place in the summer time, when its population of over eight hundred is greatly increased. There are fine level walks around the bay, to the Aros park (an open space on the site of demolished Druimfin House), and to the lighthouse on the north side. From the upper village, roads lead inland: the route we shall follow to Dervaig; a short return journey to Glengorm and its castle, from which many old roads spread out; what used to be a public road to Dervaig (now a forestry road); and another very rough track to meet our Dervaig road beyond the Mishnish lochs.

Left: Salen Bay

Above: On the Tobermory to Dervaig road: Loch Frisa, Mull's largest loch, in the distance
Below: Dervaig: described as 'the most picturesque village in the Hebrides'

Descending from 'Snake Pass' (but no snakes!) at the fourth milestone we come to the point where the very rough track from Glengorm joins ours; on the other side of the road a new track has been made to reach Loch Frisa, four miles long and the longest loch in Mull. This is another excellent fishing loch, with further access through the forestry plantations from the other end above Aros Bridge.

Yet another delightful little loch is passed, Loch Torr, artificially created by the building of a dam across the confluence of two little burns in the year 1900. There are trout in abundance – brown, rainbow, sea-trout – and the very rare chance of a salmon. Tackle and Books, Tobermory, will give you the use of a boat.

We are driving over one of the most attractive and exciting roads in Mull where the distances are short, but the miles go on for ever! The Achnadrish hill stretch, rising steeply from Loch Torr, is typical, with innumerable hairpin bends, and the same on the descent to Dervaig on the other side. From the top, however, there is a wonderful view of the moorlands and far hills. Then just over the watershed, on a small grassy hollow beside a lay-by, you will see three tiny cairns thirty feet (9m) apart: they mark off the length of the legendary leaps of an athletic and skilled swordsman of the Clan MacKinnon. He foiled the attacks of a marauding party of Macleans over from Coll by taking such memorable leaps (one of them backwards) that he sent the other team running. Just a few yards further on we come to the top of the winding descent to Dervaig village (its population about 170): before us lies a breath-taking view, a panorama of sea and land, of the steps and stairs of lava beds, and most arresting in clear weather, the tops of the hills of Harris sixty miles distant, all the low ground hidden by the curvature of the earth. At this point (as at the Mishnish lochs) we have climbed to a level of 400ft (118m).

The friendly little village of Dervaig is described as one of the most picturesque in the Hebrides; it is also a place where the old people can still be heard talking in the Gaelic tongue in the bar of the hotel. You will be told incredulous tales of the prestigious car rally held in October, when the section of road we have just followed is closed to the public – and at night – and when the timed 7½ miles of it is covered in 7½ to 8 minutes!

If several of the little cottages in the one street were thatched instead of roofed with corrugated iron, we could well be looking at the house as it was when built in the year 1800. Here, the road which crosses Mull from Salen joins our road, just at the old bridge crossing the River Bellart; this is below Kilmore church with the pencil steeple which is uncommon. Although common in Ireland, we are only familiar with one other of its kind over here, at Dunfermline, in Fife. A short distance further on, a side road crosses the five long miles over to Torloisk, ascending by the 'Pass of the Mirror' a 1:3½ gradient.

Dervaig is a good centre for walking: through the forestry plantations to Glengorm; along the Salen road to the site of the old market and the

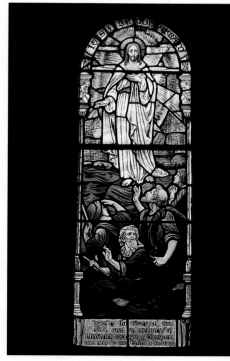

Stained glass at Kilmore Church, Dervaig

Well preserved salmon trap in the estuary of the River Bellart at Dervaig (Photo: Author)

Medieval graveslabs in the vestry of Kilninian church

'Bargain Stone' where debts were settled; or go out above the sea-loch to Quinish estate, and keeping to the right along the little roads, reach the open ground and head for Mingary – and some of the old ruins of the evictions of the past. This, too, is the way to the 'Stone Tree' of Quinish which we have already described. Before leaving Dervaig, look out to the west side of the estuary and there you will see a very well-preserved example of a 'fish trap'. It consists of a winding, level, drystone wall built from shore to shore at low tide point; at high tide the wall is covered deeply, fish drift inshore over the top of the wall and are left stranded behind it when the tide recedes. Being below the highwater mark of ordinary tides, the proprietors could claim no rights as a rule, and much to their chagrin the people could collect the fish freely.

This had been a centre of population since Neolithic times, when the standing stones you can see today above Dervaig were set up.

Our road leads on to Calgary. There is a two-mile diversion we can take to Croig – 'Cattle Inlet' – where cattle from the islands used to be landed, and in our own time 'puffers' used to come in to deliver coal for the scattered houses round about. Calgary Bay is four miles distant from Dervaig. It is one of the most scenic and popular places in Mull, a beach of white sand backed by a stretch of sheep-grazed machair land, within a curving perimeter of woodland on steep hill slopes. The beach is officially designated one of the cleanest, and the sea there the cleanest in Scotland. Above the little pier on the other side a track leads up to the ruins of Inivea, the little township that was completely cleared. No doubt it was these townspeople, and those from much of the north of Mull, who left on an emigrant ship from here.

Beyond Calgary the motorist, like Agag, must come delicately, for the road narrows for half a mile, and skirts the edge of a 100ft cliff, with blind corners, bends, and a drop to the shore under his elbow; though fortunately it is one of the less busy roads. Just past the worst section where there is a very sudden, short descent at the foot of a great rock slide towering above, there is a flat bracken-infested area between the road and the edge of the cliff. Here we can see the only cup-marked rocks in Mull (unless there are traces at Scoor, in the Ross of Mull). This was obviously a place of some ceremonial nature, perhaps even as far back as megalithic, or more probably Iron Age times; there are also wide stretches of ruins almost level with the turf. It is known as the Druids' Field.

We see a road branching off to the west: this leads to Treshnish House, formerly the property of Lady Jean Rankin who was a lady in waiting to the Queen Mother. Our track carries on for a mile or so to Haunn, consisting of a few old cottages, mostly modernised, that belonged to an old Mull family of inshore fishermen. The cliffs here featured in the film *The Eye of the Needle*; in fact other corners of Mull were also sufficiently photogenic to appear on three other films: *Madam Sin*, *I Know Where I'm Going*, and *Where Eight Bells Toll*.

Soon after we come to the gaunt, ruined schoolhouse of Reudle standing above the road, once a centre for the few houses scattered for miles around, but all gone long since. Leave the car, walk to the level of the schoolhouse, bear right and left along the same contour, and you see a valley opening towards the sea. About a mile down in the valley, near the top of the cliff, we find what are probably the two best preserved villages – or rather hamlets – from the late eighteenth century: Crakaig and Glacgugairidh ('Hollow of the Dark Grazings'). After admiring the skill of the men who fitted the smooth wall-stones, we can proceed to the edge of the steep slope, descend by a path that can still be faintly traced, cross the 100ft raised beach, and go down to the rocky shore by a steep gully in the cliff. Here, to the right, we shall see the foundations of a large still. It consisted of a 14ft

Kilninian church, Torloisk

(4.3m) diameter platform with a hemispherical hollow where a fire heated the 'black pot' and drove off the vapour that was cooled by a tiny stream dripping over the front of the cave on to the 'worm' from which the alcohol dripped. This was still operated successfully in the middle of the nineteenth century, and is still described as being of excellent quality!

Beyond Reudle the road climbs up to a watershed, then drops down – in the inevitable hairpin bends and steep gradients – to the Torloisk side. From the top we have another of those views that forces us to halt and admire, the big hills of central Mull with Ben More dominating and the islands of Ulva and Gometra, separated from the Torloisk shore by Loch Tuath, the North Loch. At the first farm buildings near the foot of the hill, look west along the hill slopes and about half a mile away you will see the outline of a well-preserved Iron Age fort, Dun Aisgean, a defensive post on top of a small mound. Still further on we come to the church of Kilninian, built in the late eighteenth century, like Kilmore at Dervaig. Here again we find some very old graveslabs and table tombs covering the graves of chiefs of the Macleans of Torloisk; one is intricately carved to mark the grave of a

woman, probably one of the wives. We have passed Torloisk House, set back amongst the usual fine fir trees that distinguish the residences of the old chiefs or more recent landowners who planted them. The hill road from Dervaig joins us on the left at the factor's house.

From there onwards for the next twelve miles the scenery is some of the most impressive in Mull: passing Ballygown Bay, and down on the shore, we can see the low walls of one of Mull's two brochs, Dun na' Gall. Halfway to Ulva ferry there is a picturesque little spot at a bridge with a fine cataract above; this drops from under the road bridge straight into the sea and is known as 'Eas Fors', an interesting combination of Gaelic and Norse, for the two words each mean 'Waterfall'. Our next stop is Ulva Ferry, where a short road runs down to the slipway.

We have already touched on the history of Ulva, that island of sad memories but with hopes for the future, and from now on our major interest is its scenery. After negotiating the hill from Ulva Ferry the road becomes less hazardous, we pass the occasional farm, and finally come to the woodlands around Killiechronan, the 'Singing Wood' where the River Ba opens to the head of Loch na Keal. Here we are joined by the short road leading from Salen and the Sound of Mull.

CENTRAL MULL

OUR ROAD, although still adventurous at a few points, is for the rest of our Mull tour reasonably level, with fewer blind corners and tortuous bends such as we experienced in the northern area among the 'Nish' and escarpment landscape of the lava fields.

We are now in the sporting centre of Mull backed by the big hills around Loch Ba, two miles in length, lying in the heart of what was the main volcanic complex. Gruline House lies among the trees, and near it the mausoleum of General Macquarie, Father of Australia as they called him, where he lies with his family; a direction post on the main road points to the little building. Just beyond Gruline we cross the old bridge spanning the River Ba built during the Clearances, and beside the road there is a right of way post indicating the way across to Glen More, a short cut much used in the old days. The path skirts the picturesque end of the loch and turns up ice-worn Glen Clachaig to the watershed at 1,000ft (303m) on the shoulder of Ben More.

The road now follows the level raised beach along Loch na Keal – there are two sheep farms on the slopes above us and the best path to the top of Ben More passes Derryguaig, the more westerly of the two. It is more of a steep walk than a climb, with the most rewarding views imaginable from the summit. A careful climber could descend the eastern face of the Ben and join the right of way we have just described.

Then without warning the road disappears round yet another corner

Left: Eas Fors, near Ulva Ferry. Note the spelling: one Gaelic word, one Norse, both meaning 'waterfall'

The 'front' garden of a cottage in Gribun

Looking across Loch Scridain to Ben More from Pennyghael

and we find ourselves in a world of rocks, the gloomy north-facing 1,000ft cliffs of Gribun above us and the road cut through the rock itself, with the rocky shore fifty feet below us. This is a dangerous half mile after very wet or frosty weather, when rock-falls are common. Thankfully, we turn back into the sunshine as the cliffs draw back and more open ground allows for some farming. In times of heavy rain the little streams falling down the cliffs are checked in the clefts and chimneys and blown back across the top like smoke.

Immediately opposite the first farm we come to is an enormous boulder standing 150 feet or so above the road: Tragedy Rock, or Creag nan Caraid, we call it. In the late eighteenth century a young couple were spending the first night after their wedding in a tiny cot-house tucked under an outcrop that deflected falling boulders. But on that night, a wild night of wind and rain the rock face split and this huge section rolled down, crushing the house and its occupants who still lie beneath this great tombstone.

Just offshore lies the island of Inch Kenneth, formerly second in sanctity to Iona itself; it is private property. It has a ruined chapel, old burying ground, a modern farm bungalow and a fine mansion house, once the property of the Mitford family. About 200 yards west of the little slipway on the Mull shore you will see several millstones still lying in the bed of hard sandstone: at one time there was a small industry here which supplied millstones, for nearly every estate had its own water mill.

As the road begins to climb along the face of the great escarpment, you will find a farm road leading down to the farm; the car can be left here. A walk of half a mile leads to the edge of the low sea-cliff where a gate in the fence allows a scramble down to the boulder beach. About a hundred yards to the left you will come to the great entrance to MacKinnon's Cave, named after the abbot who made this his sanctuary for meditation; it runs back for about a hundred yards into total darkness, and at the end, which is blocked with rockfalls, there is a huge rock table fallen from the roof. It is a cave that impressed even the great Dr Johnson. But beware: it is the home of evil spirits which are said to have caused the deaths of a party of adventurous men who sought to penetrate to the intricacies of the cave.

Make your way over the top and down Glen Seilisdair, the Iris Glen, to the sea at Loch Scridain, beside Kilfinichen church. Here a road strikes back along the shore to Tiroran House, and beyond to the isolated farms of Tavool and Burg; beyond Tiroran (now a private hotel) the road deteriorates. From there, a walk of three miles, passing Tavool and ending at Burg sheep farm, takes you into the National Trust land known as the Wilderness, the headland of Ardmeanach faced by a continuation of the high cliffs of Gribun. First you must call at Burg and report your intention to visit this area; then take the paths along the glacis of the cliffs – no more than sheep and wild goat tracks – and so to McCulloch's tree, which lies a short distance beyond the more northerly of the double waterfalls, about a mile from Burg and which we have already described. It is a fascinating place of fluted

The Coladoir river near Kinloch at the head of Loch Scridain

columns, caves and cliffs. At the point where the walker descends from the cliff paths to the rocky shore below a number of flat concentric columns can be seen on the beach, probably other fossil trees worn flat when the cliff receded. Watch the tide – as you should do at MacKinnon's Cave – and approach at half or low tide, otherwise you will be comprehensively cut off until the tide ebbs.

Return to the main road; four or five miles further on, with Ben More towering above, is the bridge over the River Coladoir at the mouth of Glen More, at Kinloch. Here we join the main road from Craignure to Iona, and leave the mountainous central area behind.

THE ROSS OF MULL

'ROS' IS THE GAELIC WORD for a far-reaching peninsula. After about three miles, just beyond the little hamlet of Pennyghael, a road climbs up to our left and crosses the moorlands for four miles to Carsaig Bay, one of the most scenic bays in Mull. It lies in an amphitheatre of 700ft (215m) cliffs, with a flat arable area above the beach of dark sand. The road dips very steeply indeed over the top of the descent; and it is far better to park the car at the top and walk down to the pier among the tall trees; as you do so, avoiding the precincts of Carsaig House, which is a private school of painting in the summertime. Keeping strictly to the shore, proceed west towards and round the high headland, and in about a mile you come to the Nun's Cave, a shallow wide cave in the sandstone measure of the cliff with masses of fossil shells, the whole topped by columnar basalts. This is a part of the old foundations of the island, dipping under the weight of lavas in the north. The cave is so-called because the nuns of Iona were said to have taken refuge there for a while after being expelled from the island at the Reformation. The monks worked the flat tidal quarry of hard sandstone in front, extracting slabs and carrying them up to the shelter of the cave where they shaped them into ornamentations, graveslabs and so on; the west wall is incised with holy symbols left by those ancient masons. The hardy walker can carry on for a further mile or so to the famous Carsaig Arches, columnar basalts worn into fantastic shapes. Those 700ft (213m) cliffs present an unbroken barrier for miles along the south coast of Mull.

Back on the main road and near the isolated church there stands a simple cairn in memory of the famous Beaton doctors of Mull, physicians first to the Lords of the Isles and then to the Macleans of Duart.

We are now approaching the granite area of the Ross. A few miles short of Bunessan village (population 150) there stands above the road on the left a monument to Mary MacDonald, a simple, uneducated Gaelic speaker who lived in this district and composed the words of that great hymn 'Child in the Manger'. Bunessan is a trim little village standing on Loch Lathaich; like Tobermory in the north it is a busy centre for the district. Here we have a crofting community, good land, and such little scattered hamlets as Uisken

A symbol carved on the wall of Nuns' Cave, Carsaig, is considered by the Ancient Monuments Commission to be the trade mark of a mason or monk who worked there, possibly in Early Christian times

Top right: The ferry crossing from Fionnphort to Iona

Bottom right: Sguabain's rock – subject of a legend from Glen More

EWEN OF THE LITTLE HEAD

In Loch Sguabain lies the small, fortified island which was the home of Ewen of the Little Head, son of the ageing chief of the Maclaines of Lochbuie. The story of how Ewen lost his head, a mixture of fact and folklore, is related later as a typical Mull story. Facing us across the loch is Cnoc Fhada, the long ridge: on the summit is the long hollow said to have been worn by the scaly body of a fearsome dragon that once crouched here, terrorising the glen as it waited for some unwary prey to appear. It was finally dispatched by the ingenuity of a certain young man, who was rewarded with the hand of the local overlord's pretty daughter. A place indeed to make you uneasy, for the ghosts come flocking out at dusk in Glen More.

Dugald MacPhail's cairn

and Ardalanish, with some fine beaches around the coast. Across the flat moor of Ardtun north of Bunessan is the strata of mudstone in the low cliffs containing the famous fossil leaves and blossoms; a large area of worn basalts can also be found near the leaf-beds.

A further five or six miles along the main road takes us to its end at Fionnphort – the white port – where there is a big car park, and the jetty for the ferry to Iona, just a mile across the Sound of Iona; the abbey and the village can be seen across the water. North of Fionnphort, a short walk takes you to an extensive quarry where for many years an attractive red or pink granite was extracted (see p23). Just north again of the quarry lies the tiny hamlet of Kintra, the other point in Mull where the black cattle used to be landed from the further islands, at Traigh na Margadh (Market Bay). Like Bunessan, Fionnphort has road connections with many little scattered hamlets and farms. In fact many of the cottages here are the holiday homes of absentee owners, or for letting in the summer.

Back now at Kinloch, and we can return to Craignure by the Glen More road; and surely in all Scotland there is no glen with such a store of history and tradition! Bare, bleak, glacier-smoothed sides, piles of moraines and scattered, ice-borne rocks, there is not a house to be seen for nearly ten miles. The focal point lies to the east of the watershed, above a valley in which lie three small lochs; the nearest is Loch Sguabain, with the little salmon river, the Lussa, flowing out of it and thence down Strath Coil, the right-angled continuation of Glen More, and on down to Loch Spelve. Stop and park above Loch Sguabain (now an excellent sea trout loch) and walk a few hundred yards down to a disused lay-by on the old road; here a huge, pointed boulder has come to rest, known as Clach Sguabain, or Sguabain's stone. This gentleman was one of the Fingalain giants, and legend relates that he was standing here minding his own business one day, when this boulder was hurled at him, for no recorded reason, by Nicol, another of the giants who was standing some way away on the shore of Loch Spelve; and over there you can see the rock that Sguabain hurled back in retaliation.

At Ardura crossroads, at the estuary of the Lussa, there stands a handsome monument to Dugald MacPhail, the most famous of Mull's many poets and storytellers who composed and wrote the words of that famous song *The Isle of Mull*, a verse of which appears at the beginning of this book.

The side road runs steeply over the Ardura hill and on to Loch Buie, the 'Yellow Loch', passing Loch Uisg and a jungle of rhododendrons, and emerging on the open windswept shore. Moy Castle, ancient stronghold of the Maclaines of Lochbuie, can be seen along the shoreline to the left. Please keep to the shore and respect the privacy of the modern mansion that was built to replace the early fifteenth-century castle. On the flat plain inland there is a splendid example of a stone circle. The right of way from Carsaig along the shoreline ends here, but if the energetic explorer cares to cover the three rough miles to the southern point of the Laggan peninsula, he will be able to explore the intricacies of Lord Lovat's Cave.

On returning to the crossroads at Ardura, take a walk along the old woodland road beside the River Lussa until you come to a low bluff with a nice salmon pool below: this is called the Pedlar's Pool, and on the bank you will see a simple cairn surmounted by an iron cross in Celtic design bearing the inscription 'John Jones, died 1st April 1891'. This is the grave of a pedlar who gave up his rounds to nurse a family in the Ross of Mull smitten with the smallpox, a disease regarded with almost superstitious horror by the people then. Finally the pedlar resumed his rounds, but by the time he reached this point he was severely infected with the disease and died here; he is buried along with his pack.

Our next stop on the way home is another little hamlet, Lochdonhead. Just before passing it, notice another road which crosses a bridge over a narrow arm of Loch Don: this leads to Grass Point which was once Mull's busy main ferry to Oban and the chief export point for the cattle driven through Mull along the old drove roads.

Last, but certainly not least, is Duart Castle, one of the buildings of greatest interest in the island. It is reached by the side road marked 'Kilpatrick', and constitutes a diversion of two miles or so. Duart is of course the home of the chief of the Macleans 'of Dowart and Morvern', restored from its ruinous condition in 1912.

Craignure Bay opens up once more before us, and sadly we are at our journey's end – MacBraynes' fine big 100-car ferry is waiting at the pier. Or is it? Shall we just carry on back to Tobermory and savour Mull's attractions once again, and at more leisure, to appreciate the details?

Caber tossing at the Isle of Mull Highland Games

SPORT AND LEISURE PURSUITS

MULL HAS A DIVERSITY of other attractions of which angling must be considered one of the most important. Every loch and rivulet has its stock of native brown trout, with imported rainbow trout well established in some of the lochs. Great fun can be had stalking the little trout along the burn sides, a pursuit which is even more exciting by the loch side or out in a boat, waiting for one of the big fish to take your fly, exploding like a depth charge as it does so. As we become older the lure of angling is not so much the heavy basket as the enjoyment of the finer art of enticing a fish in a difficult location, calling for skill. Salmon and sea-trout are now much more scarce, a situation entirely due to international disinterest as regards the safeguarding of the sea lanes followed by the fish in their progress towards our rivers. Nonetheless if the sea-trout are 'in', a thrilling time can be had fishing below highwater mark at high tides at the mouths of rivers and burns.

From Tobermory, some of the best sea-angling in Britain is available, in fact bookings for a year ahead are quite common. Some incredible fish have been caught in the Sound of Mull north of Tobermory, that are records for the British Isles.

GOLF

The long-established golf course at Tobermory run by the Western Isles Hotel may not rival Gleneagles or Birkdale because it is short, only nine holes, but its hazards are challenging and for the straight hitter it is an enjoyable, well trimmed course of 2,460yd (2,249m), par 64; a new clubhouse was built in 1991. There is another club at Craignure, the re-incarnation of a rough course that existed in the 1920s, which has great possibilities.

Botany, geology, archaeology: there is something for everyone with items of special interest that attract the experts too. We have already indicated that the birdlife is of phenomenal variety and interest, and it is said that you have missed one of the greatest sights in Scotland if you omit to see the puffins on Lunga in the Treshnish Islands. These islands are sea-girt plateaux created from the eroded levels of ancient lava flows, in winter exposed to the driving mists and spray of the Atlantic storms, in summer and fine weather basking in seas of Hebridean blue. From Mull their silhouettes are reminiscent of high-bowed ships eternally sailing line ahead into the distance. The reefs and rocky shelves are the breeding places of the grey seal in autumn, and of course this is a bird sanctuary with a bewildering variety of birds.

Lunga is the largest of these islands; the ruins of two small cottages can be seen on it, with a small area nearby where the fishermen would grow a few potatoes when staying there during the fishing season. On the west side stands the Harp Rock – Dun Cruit – so named because of its resemblance to a harp when observed from certain angles. It is cut off from the cliff by an angled chasm about a hundred feet deep, the white-foamed Atlantic rollers surging in at its foot. The isolated top is partly grass, and riddled with the nesting burrows of puffins whose young, the 'gugas' as they were called, were once collected and salted down as a winter delicacy. To collect them from the Harp Rock, the fishermen would carry up the mast of their skiff, lower it across the chasm which was about 15ft (4.5m) wide at its narrowest part, and then shin across with net bags hanging round neck and waist which they would fill with gugas and eggs.

Cairnburg Mor was a fortress-island from the thirteenth century, made all but impregnable because of its defensive walling round the top of the cliff, and its steep access path down which rocks could be rolled from a stockpile at the top thus sweeping away attackers. There is a little-known story about the island: just below the edge of the cliff, with the sea surging below, there is a projecting rocky shelf known as 'Urraigh Ailean nan Sop' translated as 'Allan of the Straw's Eyrie' (the origin of that nickname is another story). One day Allan, who was a reformed pirate and by then chief of the Macleans of Torloisk, was visiting the island in company with MacNeill of Barra and his pretty daughter, together with a few retainers. Fascinated by the girl, Allan managed to separate her from the party, and standing near the edge of the cliff, began to make coarse and unwelcome advances. Seeing the girl's distress, one of her servants rushed up and pushed Allan right over the cliff edge. Fortunately he landed on this rocky projection, from which the servant helped him up – but only on condition that Allan would mend his ways!

Staffa is an island that needs no introduction, except that the original name of Fingal's Cave is so much more descriptive in the original Gaelic, which means 'The Melodious Cave,' a point well appreciated by Mendelssohn.

All the islands can be visited starting from centres in Mull; little cruise

Left: The Coladoir river, at the head of Loch Scridain, with the peaks of Cruachan Dearg and Corra-Bheinn behind

Overleaf: Fingal's Cave, Staffa

boats are used, manned by experienced seamen – but they will not take a chance with the weather. Pony trekking is available at several other centres, and one scenic track in particular comes to mind: along the shores of picturesque Loch Ba through the woodlands, by the path that took us over the shoulder of Ben More by Glen Clachaig.

Regarding indoor pursuits, there are frequent ceilidh concerts and dances; also craft shops are a form of entertainment, with a selection of quality items made on the island, from silverwork to woollens. The Tobermory museum is certainly well worth a visit, with its increasing number of exhibits; and conveniently beside it is the long-established distillery that welcomes visiting parties when it is in production.

Mull Pottery, Tobermory

Over at Dervaig is situated the former site of Britain's smallest professional theatre, featuring in the Guinness Book of Records, that closed in 2006 to reopen on a new site in Druimfin 2008. Also at Dervaig there is a tableau showing the homes of a cottar and of a tacksman as they would have looked back in the days of the Clearances.

Agricultural shows, clay pigeon shooting, flower shows, dog trials, highland games, even a school of painting: there's always something going on. In the bay we can often see several dozen yachts – it is a great yachting centre.

We could go on forever, but suffice to say: meet the local people, and though you will be regarded at first with a speculative eye, you will soon find lasting friendships.

Former site of Mull Little Theatre, Dervaig

6 IONA AND SAINT COLUMBA

IONA AND ST COLUMBA are of such significance that they warrant full treatment in a separate book; here we can give only a brief general summary. Iona is now a busy, sunny holiday island with bays of dazzling white sand and green translucent water. There are fine views towards the mountains of Mull, which not only protect the island from the worst of the east winds, but also attract the rain clouds from the west before they have time to precipitate their heaviest rain on the fertile island, which thus has a better record of sunshine than Mull. It stretches 3 miles (4.8km) from north to south and 1¹/₂ miles from east to west; 2,000 acres (800ha) in extent, rising to 332ft (101m) at Dun I, its highest point. There is a crofting community, the population of between sixty and eighty concentrated in the little village near the abbey, connected with the ferry-port Fionnphort in Mull across the Sound of Iona.

Iona, the island of St Columba, is steeped in history and tradition. Here we can see 'the moon on royal tombstones gleam', and read in coats-of-arms the stories of men who fought, and preached and died from the dawn of Christianity in Scotland. We can still feel that intangible

The Bishop's House

Left: John's cross

Overleaf: St Oran's chapel

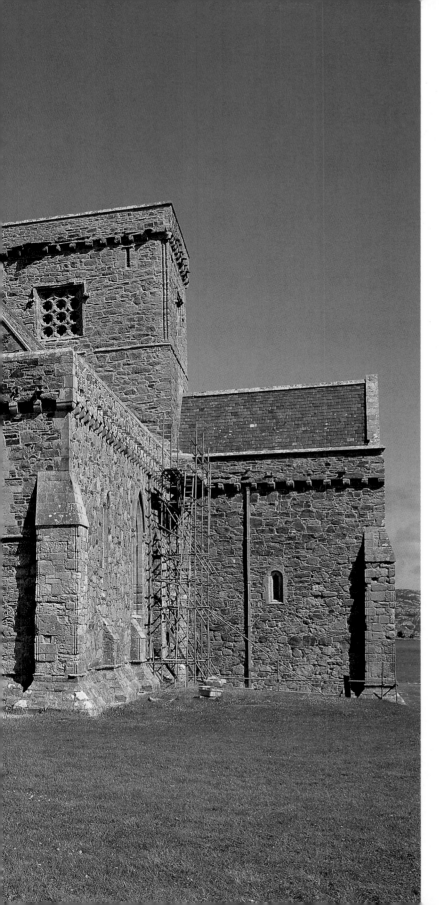

atmosphere so well conveyed in the words of the great Dr Johnson: 'We are now treading that illustrious Island, which was once the luminary of the Caledonian regions, whence the savage clans and roving barbarians derived the benefits of knowledge and the blessings of religion . . . that man is little to be envied whose . . . piety would not grow warmer among the ruins of Iona'.

The significance of Iona began in AD563 when Columba, with his twelve disciples, landed near the marble quarries at Port a Churaich, Port of the Coracle, in the south of the island. A coracle in those days could be quite a large craft, made of stout wickerwork covered with hides and well caulked. On the shore there are strange piles of stones, said to have been raised by the monks as penance for some misdemeanour. As Pennant said pawkily during his visit, 'To judge by some of those heaps, it is no breach of charity to think there were among them enormous sinners!'

St Columba, a prince of Ireland and descendant of Niall of the Nine Hostages, devoted his life to religion and was a follower of St Patrick. He did not come to Scotland originally as a missionary, as is sometimes thought, but as a self-imposed penance, a sad man seeking voluntary banishment after a well-meaning but stubborn action that led to bloodshed. What happened was this:

One of his colleagues, Fenian, returned from Rome with a copy of the first Vulgates to reach Ireland, a simplified translation of the Gospels. Always a seeker after truth and

93

COLUMBA'S LAW

Columba would not allow either woman or cow to be upon Iona, for as he is reported to have said: 'Where there is a cow there is a woman, and where there is a woman there is mischief.' Workers at the abbey had to leave their womenfolk on Eilean nam Ban, 'Women's Island', which lies across the front of the little anchorage called the 'Bullhole', just below the Tormore granite quarries. Ancient ruins of little houses can still be seen on the island. He is also said to have banished frogs and snakes from Iona, although there are plenty just across the Sound of Iona in Mull.

Pages 92–3: The abbey on Iona, with Martin's cross in the foreground

simplicity, Columba asked for a copy, but was refused. Determined to have his way, he secretly managed to secure a copy; but when this became known he was ordered to surrender it (could this be the first recorded breach of copyright?). This he refused to do, even when the High King intervened and insisted. Columba was defiant, and the outcome was a bitter dispute which ended in a pitched battle between the two factions. Columba and his supporters prevailed, but he was so overcome with remorse at the bloodshed he had caused that he went into voluntary exile.

He landed first in the Garvelloch Islands in the Firth of Lorne, the 'Isles of the Sea'; but as he was still able to see the distant hills of Ireland, he left, and moved on to Iona, from where he could no longer see Ireland.

Columba was, however, no humble monk to retire into obscurity. Restless and militant in character, and finding himself in a pagan community he was able to give his missionary instincts full scope. First of all he laid out an area of land dedicated to church activities (it can still be distinguished from the air) in which he founded an abbey with all the necessary outbuildings. At first its construction was primitive, but as time went on skilled monkish masons replaced wood, wickerwork and turf with stone. The abbey when finished was richly ornamented; in fact some of the details are reminiscent of Notre Dame, in Paris, where grotesque impish faces were designed to scare off the powers of evil.

Iona had been a centre of pagan worship, however, and even Columba is said to have yielded to supernatural forces. As the story goes, he was held back from completing the building of what was to become the little chapel of St Oran until a living person had been buried in the foundations. His friend Oran volunteered to become the sacrifice and was duly covered up; but Columba so regretted his loss that he asked that Oran's face be uncovered for a last farewell. But as soon as the earth was removed, Oran began to speak, describing the Heaven and Hell he had seen in such blasphemous terms that Columba hastily ordered 'Earth, earth, in the mouth of Oran that he may speak no more'!

The precincts grew, attracting pilgrims and scholars from distant places. Few traces remain today, but a line of standing stones stretched from Grass Point to Iona marking the 'Pilgrims' Way'. The sacred soil of Iona also became the last resting place of forty-eight kings of Scotland from Fergus II to MacBeth, besides kings of Norway and France, and even an archbishop of Canterbury, as reported by Martin Martin, that great traveller. Just south of Grass Point is Port nam Marbh, the Port of the Dead, where many of the great dignitaries were landed and carried by their cortège to Iona, ending up by following the Street of the Dead (part is still visible) to the burying place in Reilig Odhrain, Oran's burying place beside the abbey. There used to be a railed enclosure round the line of plain slabs marking the graves, but sadly, the site has been lost within the last few years on the plea that the slabs had to be removed and placed under cover in order to preserve them. Surely, however, the sacredness of the soil is of so much more importance than the

unadorned slabs? We feel the site could well have been identified with an appropriate signboard.

It is remarkable how those people from so long ago had an instinctive awareness of the permanence of Iona which we have explained geologically. A very old Gaelic prophecy was translated and paraphrased by Mr Smith, of Campbeltown:

> Seven years before that awful day
> When time shall be no more
> A watery deluge will o'ersweep
> Hibernia's mossy shore.
>
> The green-clad Isla, too, shall sink
> While with the great and good
> Columba's happy isle will rear
> Her towers above the flood.

Columba was by no means the first missionary to become established in Scotland, and others were perhaps more effective in their local environment; Columba and his disciples however spread the word throughout Scotland, converting the king of the Picts at Inverness, and crossing over to Scandinavia, even as far as the Rhine Valley.

In connection with Columba's visit to Inverness to the Pictish king Adamnan wrote in his *Life of Columba* seventy years after the death of the saint, describing what appears to be the first sighting of the legendary

Overleaf: The nunnery

95

creature known as the Loch Ness monster. As the party came to the River Ness, they found a number of local people bewailing the death of one of them who had just been killed by a great water beast. Columba nevertheless sent one of his servants swimming across to obtain a boat for the convenience of the missionaries – and the swimmer was also attacked by this great creature; but Columba, approaching the bank and holding up his arm, 'forbade' it, whereupon it 'withdrew as if drawn by ropes'.

It is remarkable how much of the lore of St Columba is still preserved in Mull; one might think that merely decades had intervened instead of centuries. At Salen, on the Sound of Mull, there is a little rivulet called the 'Burn of the Sermon' where a chapel was built, but the quality of the water was not acceptable. People will point out to you the bluff on which Columba stood to give his sermon; and indeed the story goes that there was not a great attendance.

Then in the year 806 came the first visit of the piratical Norsemen, seeking gold and plunder, who put many of the monks to death. Yet again, and finally in 986, they wrecked the work of years and slaughtered the people in their hunt for plunder. However, in spite of those piratical activities, Christianity was slowly adopted by the Norsemen, and by the time their domination had ended in the thirteenth century, the Bishop of Iona was being ordained at Trondheim in Norway, and Iona was spared.

Columba, seeking always after simplicity, founded the Celtic Church, or the Church of the Culdees ('Servants of God') with centres throughout Scotland – the foundations of one such chapel can be seen under the flagstones of the nave of Dunfermline Abbey. While the Church of Rome was the Mother Church, the Celtic Church differed in certain doctrinal details, and was finally suppressed by King David in 1144.

This 'University of the North' and 'Cradle of Christianity in Scotland' as it became known, was a centre of the arts: handsome carvings, manuscripts, ornamental graveslabs, Celtic crosses, all were the work of the monks and craftsmen; but greatest of all was that handsome Book of Kells, prepared in about the year 800 – this was Celtic art at its best.

The asceticism of Columba was long past when, in 1203, Reginald of the MacDonalds of the Isles built a nunnery for the Order of the Black Nuns, as well as a Benedictine abbey. However, some of the glory of Iona was being overshadowed by the rise of Dunfermline as a royal city, and also as a more convenient place of interment for the great. The final eclipse of Iona came with the Reformation and the passing of the Act of 1561 by the Scottish parliament 'for demolishing all the abbeys of monks and friars, and for suppressing whatsoever monuments of idolatrie were remaining in the realm'.

Iona became a target for bigoted and vindictive vandalism, worse even than the acts of the pagan Norsemen. Buildings were demolished; of the 360 carved crosses said to have been displayed, only three survive today. Worst of all, the great library was sacked, and its treasures of art and literature going back to the days of St Columba were all destroyed. Fortunately the Book of

Top left: Effigy of Abbot Dominic, abbot of the Benedictine monastery of Iona from 1421 to 1465. He initiated the rebuilding of the abbey church

Bottom left: The tomb of John MacKinnon, the last abbot of Iona, AD1500

The ferry from Fionnphort on Mull across the mile-wide sound of Iona (Photo: Author)

A leisurely drive may be had to the Abbey instead of the quarter-mile walk – or a drive around the island – by this horse-drawn carriage (Photo: Author)

Kells was saved and taken to Ireland, and a few of the treasures that could conveniently be handled were taken by the fleeing monks to Dublin, Paris, Rome and elsewhere. Few remained in Scotland, though one, fortunately, which did, was the beautiful stipple-ornamented Brecbennoch or Breakbeannoch – the 'beautiful stippled object', a sacred reliquary of St Columba which was carried before the Scottish troops at Bannockburn and is now to be seen in the Scottish Museum of Antiquities in Edinburgh. Graves and sepulchres were ravaged; even the church bells were taken away.

Tradition had it that some of the treasures were hidden on Cairnburg Mor in the Treshnish Islands, but were found by Cromwell's troops and destroyed. However, could some have been missed? Are there fragments of those ancient items still to be found?

Succeeding the MacDonalds, the Macleans of Duart became the owners of Iona, now a sacred desert; then finally, as they lost their possessions in the island of Mull, the island came into the hands of the Dukes of Argyll, where it remains to this day.

Some reconstruction was carried out in 1855 by the Society of Antiquarians; however, in 1899 the 8th Duke of Argyll made over the buildings to the Church of Scotland for the use of all Christian denominations, hoping that restorations might be carried out. The local community carried out restoration work for years as far as finances and circumstances permitted, until the Iona Community took over in 1938. Volunteers from all trades gave their time and services during the holiday periods, inspired by the enthusiastic leadership of the Rev George MacLeod, who was deservedly created Lord MacLeod of Fuinary in 1968 for his work. Now the abbey buildings have returned to their simple beauty, with smooth walls of pink granite, woodwork donated by Norway, and both materials and cash gifts received from all over the world.

Care and maintenance of the abbey falls on the Trustees of Iona Abbey Limited, but as it is a scheduled ancient monument, all work is directed by the government body Historic Scotland; and anxious as it is to preserve the traditional appearance, there have been some departures in details which in time might well alter the original appearance. A visit to Iona is the culmination of the exploration of Mull. In spite of an unavoidable veneer of sophistication, we can still follow in the footsteps of Columba, stand where he stood on Dun I from which he could no longer see his native land, and feel something of the atmosphere that prompted the poet Yeats to write:

And I shall have some peace there, for peace comes dropping slow,
Dropping from the veils of the morning to where the cricket sings;
There midnight's all a-glimmer and noon a purple glow,
And evening full of the linnet's wings.
I will arise and go now, for always night and day
I hear lake water lapping with low sounds on the shore,
When I stand on the roadway, or on the pavement gray
I hear it in the deep heart's core.

7 THE STORY OF THE HEADLESS HORSEMAN

A CERTAIN GAELIC SONG proclaims: 'Morvern for swordplay, Mull for a song', and to this we might add '. . . and a story', for there were many gifted storytellers in Mull; and indeed they had no shortage of material, with facts, folklore, history and superstition to draw upon. One of the most popular stories concerns the Maclaines of Lochbuie and involves a fearsome ghost, a fairy woman, folklore and genuine history.

The Macleans of Lochbuie stem from the senior line of the Duart Macleans, the progenitor being Hector Reaganach, younger brother of Lachlan Libanach. However, all that interests us is what happened in the year 1538 between John, 5th chief of Lochbuie and his only son and heir Eoghann a 'Chinn Bhig, Ewen – or Hugh – of the Little Head, and its sequel. Really, the story should be related in the original Gaelic, whose nuances, asides, and vivid descriptions cannot be translated into more prosaic English.

Now, Ewen was married to a daughter of MacDougall of Lorne, a greedy ambitious wife who constantly nagged him into pressing his father for more and more of the Lochbuie lands. Generous as the chief had been on every occasion, he drew the line when Ewen was goaded into demanding the residue of the estates. Ewen was met with a blunt refusal and in spite of unfilial threats, old John was adamant. Nothing was left but an armed confrontation between the two and their supporters. John had as his ally the shrewd chief of the MacLeans of Duart, who had acquisitive ambitions.

In those days disputes of this nature were settled on the principle of a mass duel, both sides agreeing to fight it out at a pre-determined time and place.

When exploring Glen More earlier the fortress-home of Ewen was pointed out, situated on the little island in Loch Sguabain, the nearest of the three lochs that curve into the glen branching off towards Lochbuie to the south. There are conflicting opinions about the location of the fight: some say it was four miles to the west, near Craig, where bones were found in a grassy knowe; we suggest that it is more logical to identify the place as Blar na Sguabain, the flat ground to the south of where the river Lussa emerges from the loch – our own later researches would support this.

Legend had it that on the day before the confrontation Ewen was riding past a little stream when suddenly he saw before him a fairy woman dressed in green, washing blood-stained clothes in the water of the burn. With all the deference due to the Little People, Ewen approached, and enquired of her if she would be prepared to prophesy the outcome of tomorrow's fight. She did so in strange words: 'At your morning meal before the fight, if your servant fails to place butter on the table and you have to ask for it, you will be defeated' – and with that she vanished.

With so much on his mind Ewen forgot all about this – until the following morning when he found there was no butter before him. Apprehensive, but presenting a bold front, he led his followers into the fight, which became indeed a bitter struggle. Seeing his followers beginning to be hard pressed, he urged his steed into the thick of the fight; but when he was involved with several assailants, another swung his broadsword at Ewen's unprotected neck and severed his head completely from his body.

That, of course, ended the fight. Its feet jammed in the stirrups, Ewen's headless corpse was carried eastward for two miles by his terrified horse (romantically described as his 'black charger', but probably a hardy Highland pony). It splashed across the shallows above the Falls of Lussa, clambered up the steep slope and drew up exhausted at the top, at which point Ewen's body slipped to the ground. Now, if the fight had taken place over at Craig, could the horse have bolted for the six intervening miles and crossed the Lussa twice? We prefer the Blar na Sguabain theory.

Ewen's followers marked the spot with a tiny cairn among the heather. It is remarkable how the story and the location of the cairn were handed down for centuries. When we were researching the story, we asked the late Seton Gordon, who was one of the greatest authorities on West Highland folklore, if he had any information. His reply was that as far as he knew, the site was known to only one man, who lived in Fionnphort but who had shown him the location. Seton Gordon gave exact directions: search, he advised, below the lowest of the scattered buildings of ruined Torness (beside the main Glen More road) – go down the faint path for about 150 yards to where it forks: the one to the left is to the Falls of Lussa just below, the other continues down to the ford – now a footbridge – across the Lussa. Just fifty yards along the right fork you will see the tiny cairn buried in the heather at the very top of the slope from the river.

We were thrilled to come across this very spot just as directed, and have raised the height of the little cairn by adding a stone every time we have passed.

Ewen's body was buried here for a day or two before being carried to his home; when his hunting dog saw the body of its dead master it is said that the shock caused every hair to fall off its body.

Ever after Ewen's death, his uneasy ghost, mounted on his horse, haunts the roads of Mull between dusk and dawn, seeking revenge on any Maclean of Duart he may meet. Beside Loch Ba you will see a large tree trunk

Left: Beinn nan Gabhar from the Scarisdale river valley

103

still showing signs of life: here, they say, a Maclean fought the ghost all night, warding him off with one hand while he grasped a young sapling for support with the other. By the time the cock crew and the ghost had to retire to the Shades, the sapling had been torn almost horizontal – and so it still grows today: sideways!

Ewen's ghost is said to ride furiously around Moy Castle when a Lochbuie chief is about to die. Alas, the castle and estate fell into the hands of creditors who foreclosed when a more modern chief missed the deadline for paying the instalment of a massive loan by only a few hours.

Beaton cross, near Pennyghael, erected in memory of the famous Beaton doctors of the Middle Ages

In modern times we have noticed that alleged confrontations with the ghost appear to coincide with closing times at the various hotel bars. Of course in the dusk such apparitions as stray horses, cattle or sheep can quite understandably be mistaken for less tangible subjects . . .

Meanwhile, what happened to John, the elderly 5th chief, victor of the fight at Blar na Sguabain? Unwisely he had accepted the help of his cunning relative, Maclean of Duart, for which he now had to pay dearly: for Duart, seeing the Lochbuie chief now without an heir, took over the estate, seized John, and had him imprisoned on the fortress-island of Cairnburg Mor, quite alone except for the company of a middle-aged housekeeper-servant, and left in isolation except for the occasional visit of a boat bringing supplies.

The unexpected then happened: it was reported by the boatmen after one visit that the woman was in the family way, undoubtedly through liaison with the chief. Duart was alarmed, for if a male child were born he would be heir to Lochbuie, for illegitimacy did not preclude a son from the title in the absence of another legitimate heir. Leaving John in his lonely prison, Duart had the woman brought to where she could be kept under observation by a doctor and a nurse, who were instructed to ensure that no male child would survive.

While the doctor was temporarily absent, twins were born, a boy and a girl. Hastily the sympathetic nurse concealed the boy and had him rushed to the MacGillivray family in remote Glen Cannel, at the head of Loch Ba. Being told that only a girl had been born, Duart's fears were allayed, believing there could be no disputing of his retention of the Lochbuie estate.

Brought up by a devoted foster mother, the boy, known as Murachadh Gearr, or 'Dumpy Murdoch' on account of his short but powerful stature, grew to manhood, knowing his true identity and determined to return sometime to his Lochbuie inheritance, and be revenged on Maclean of Duart. Crossing to Ireland and meeting many kindred spirits, he was befriended by the Earl of Antrim, who on hearing Murdoch's story promised to give him every possible help. So Murdoch set off for Mull with a small party, knowing that once his presence was known, the clansmen would rally to his side.

As he was cautiously observing the defences of Moy Castle he dislodged a stone, making a noise which alarmed a woman who was busy milking a cow, and causing her to exclaim 'God be with you, Murdoch!' The young man then revealed himself, and asked who the Murdoch was whom she had addressed. He was her loved foster-son, she replied, now far away and missed sorely. Murdoch immediately recognised her as his MacGillivray foster-mother, and identified himself, to her joy. Her husband, she said, was now a member of the garrison defenders, and Duart's son and his wife were staying in the castle.

Murdoch explained his intention to reclaim his true inheritance, and presently the woman suggested a simple plan for re-taking the castle: Line up your men at the entrance door, she advised, late tonight when the men are all inside. I shall let loose the calves, which have been separated from their mothers, and when they meet up there will be a great disturbance while the mothers are seeking their own calf, a noise that will waken the whole garrison and bring out the men to set things right. Kill them as they come out.

But what about your husband? enquired the thoughtful Murdoch. To this she replied in a Gaelic phrase that is something of a saying: 'Let the tail go with the hide!'

Everything worked out as planned and the defenders were eliminated. But Murdoch, now a courteous opponent, allowed Duart's son and his wife to depart in dignity and peace. Of course, the Duart chief was both alarmed and perplexed at the report that a claimant had appeared for the chiefship of Lochbuie, until someone explained the circumstances. At once he called his men together to confront the young claimant.

On the night before the fight, Murdoch and one companion slipped through the lines of the opposing Macleans, to where the Duart chief was sound asleep. Murdoch gently laid his own fine sword beside the hand of the sleeper. When Duart awakened and recognised the sword, and realised how his life had been spared, he was overcome with remorse and made peace with Murdoch; and they lived in harmony until the death of Murdoch in 1586.

Useful Information and Places to Visit

The still house at Tobermory Distillery

Tourist Information

Main Street, Tobermory
Tel: 0870 720 0625 Branch Office, Craignure
Tel: 01680 812377
Information and advice on Mull, and Scotland generally; accommodation bookings, maps, books, local excursions, cruises, travel tickets. Bureau de Change. Films, souvenirs and local craft products.
The area centre of Argyll Tourist Board Ltd is at Albany Street, Oban PA34 4AR
Tel: 01631 563122   Fax: 01631 564273
All general information is also available here.

Ferry Services: Mull – Mainland

All run by Caledonian MacBrayne
Head Office, Ferry Terminus, Gourock PA19 1QP
Tel: 01475 650100   Fax: 01475 637607

Oban/Craignure
Advance bookings essential. 3–5 sailings on weekdays, 2 on Sundays (approx. 45 minutes). Tel: 01631 562285

Lochaline (Movern)/Fishnish
Advance bookings not required. 11 sailings Monday to Saturday, 4 on Sundays.

Ardnamurchan/Morvern/Tobamory
Advance bookings essential. 1–5 sailings daily.
Tel: 01972 500208

Fionnphort (Mull)/Iona
Advance bookings not required. Up to 10 sailings Monday to Saturday, 4–5 on Sundays. No motor cars.

Places to Visit

Aros Castle (ruins)
Overlooking Aros Bay, near Salen. Former major strong-hold of the Lord of the Isles.

Clydesdale Bank PLC
20 Main Street, Tobermory PA75 6NY Tel: 0845 782 6818
Banking facilities, plus travelling bank that serves the island.

Duart Castle, Near Craignure,
Tel: 01680 812309 thirteenth century home of the chief of the Clan Mclean, rebuilt in 1912. Ancient keep, dungeons, items of clan and Mull history. Scouting memorabilia collected by late chief when Chief Scout. Open daily, 10.30am to 6pm, May to mid-October.

Dunara Castle (ruins)
Near Glengorm, Strong scattered defences on small plateau above shore. Once clan centre of the MacKinnons of Mishnish.

Glengorm Castle
Private residence, five miles away from Tobermory. Magnificent setting, facing Western Hebridean islands.

Innemore School of Painting
Innemore Lodge, Pennyghael PA70 6HD
Tel: 01681 704201 Magnificent setting: open May to September.

Iona: Restored Abbey, Reilig Odhran
Tel: 01681 700404 Burial place of the early Scottish and Norwegian Kings – very old Celtic crosses, antiques. Tranquil and restful island, marble quarries, caves, geological, birdlife, full details from Iona Community, The Abbey, PA76 6SQ

Island of Ulva

Tel: 01688 500226/500264 Two minutes by ferry from Loch Tuath. Dotted with ruins from nineteenth century Clearances. Land of the Clan MacQuarrie for 600 years. Home of the forefathers of David Livingstone and Lt. Gen. Lachlan Macquarie, 'Father of Australia'. Extensive columnar basalts on SE shore. Visitor's centre, walks e.t.c.

Isle of Staffa

Unique columnar basaltic formations, Fingal's Cave and others. Local cruises from Fionnphort, Ulva Ferry, Dervaig, allowing time ashore. Been in National Trust care since 1986. Cruise details available from Information Centre, Tobermory.

Moy Castle (ruins)

Well presented ruins at Lochbuie. No admittance because of dangerous stonework. Medieval home of the chief of Clan Maclaine, an early off-shoot of the Macleans of Duart.

Mull Motor Car Rally

Annually, early October, since the 1960s, attracting up to 130 rally drivers including some of Britain's best. Unique concession of using public roads.

Mull Museum, Tobermory

Tel: 01688 302493/302020 Mull's history in artefacts and memorabilia. Open April to October, Monday to Friday 10am to 4pm; 10am to 1pm on Saturdays.

Mull Railway

Old Pier Station, Craignure Tel: 01680 812494 Craignure to Torosay Castle. Only public railway in the Hebrides. A private venture opened 1984. 10 1/4 in gauge; 11/2 miles; leisurely 15 minute journey, spectacular sights. Timetables e.t.c from Old Pier Station.

Pennygown Chapel (ruin)

Well preserved ruin. Typical pre-Reformation chapel near Salen. One of fourteen similar chapels in Mull; interesting grave slabs beside the building.

The Old Byre, Dervaig

Tableau – interior of cottar's home and that of a better-off tacksman in the early nineteenth century. Period furnishings and displays, crafts e.t.c. open Easter to October.

Tobermory Distillery

Tel: 01688 302645 Founded 1798. Visitors' centre, guided tours Monday to Friday 10am to 5pm, Easter to September (or by appointment).

Torosay Castle

Craignure, Tel: 01680 812421 Family home built in baronial style by David Bryce in the nineteenth century. Interesting family records, magnificent 12-acre gardens, statue walk e.t.c. Open daily, 10.30am to 5.30pm, May to mid-October. Gardens open 9am to 7pm in summer and during daylight hours in winter.

Treshnish Islands

3 miles off north-west Mull. Bird sanctuary, breeding place for grey seals, fantastic displays of assorted bird species, especially during May and June. Strange Harp Rock on Lunga. Near-impregnable, cliff-gert island fortress of Cairnburg Mor. Cruises as for Staffa.

Whale/Dolphin Watch Cruises

Garadh Mor Dervaig, Isle of Mull PA75 6QW
Tel: 01688 400264
Whale watching and wildlife cruises on motor vessel taking up to 12 passengers (day trips).

There are interests in Mull to suit every taste, both outdoors and indoors. The following list gives some idea of the variety, and detailed information is always available at the Information Centre.

The Isle of Mull Silver Company, Tobermory

Sporting and Outdoors

Trout and salmon fishing, Sea angling, Golf, Pony trekking, Bird Watching, Sheep Dog trials, Agricultural Shows, Clay pigeon shoots, Cruising, Yachting, Walking, Antiquities, Bus tours, Good garage facilities

Indoors

Ceilidhs/concerts, Galleries, Museum, Distillery, Theatre, Gold and silver crafts, Enamel ware, Jewellery, Painting, Pottery, Weaving

Sheep shearing at Balemeanach Farm, Gribun

PLACE NAMES AND THEIR PRONUNCIATION

The place names of Mull are of either Gaelic/Norse or pure Gaelic, which is the second oldest language in Europe. It originated in the Middle East, was brought with the Celts along the northern Mediterranean and extreme western Europe to Ireland, and finally came to Scotland with the Celtic-Scots. Broadly, the examples given below are very local, and the original word-form and even their meanings have been changed or lost as a result of being passed on by word of mouth, with few written records, over the centuries.

An attempt to master the accepted names of local topography can establish an even greater affinity with the local people in Mull. As a general rule, emphasis falls on the first syllable: *Oh*-ban, not O-*ban*; *Der*-vaig, not Der-*vaig*; *Cal*-gary, not Cal-*garry*. The 'r' sound is em-phasised, and vowels not clipped, but drawn out.

The 'ch' sound, such as in that stumbling block 'loch', is not easy in the flatter English tongue. Without being facetious, this sound can be achieved by a slight clearing of the upper throat, with lips open and tongue against the lower teeth. It can usually be slurred as an aspirated 'h', especially before a vowel: 'acha' (a field) can be pronounced as 'ah-ha'; 'acharonich' (field of bog myrtle) - 'aharonny'; but never, never, speak of a 'lock' - try to slur the word to 'lawh'.

The author's interpretation of Mull names is as strictly authentic as his long local residence can achieve. The purist may disagree, but the object is to help strangers through basic simplicity.

Place Name	Pronunciation	Meaning
Achnadrish	Ahhna-*dreesh*	Field of Brambles
Aisgean	*Aish*gin (hard 'g')	
Aline	*Ah*lin	Beautiful (loch)
Allt Airidh nan Chaisteal	Alt airy nan Hastle	Burn of the Castle Shieling
Ardalanish	Ard*ala*nish	
Ardmeanach	Ard *mee-an* ah	Middle Headland
Ardura	Ar*joo*ra	
Ballachulish	Balla*hoo*lish	Township in the Narrows
Beag	Bake	Small
Breakbeannoch	Brekbeyanna	Blessed speckled object
Buie	Booie	Yellow
Bunessan	Bun*essa*n	Foot of the cataract
Caliach	*Call*yah	Old woman
Calgary	*Cal*gary	Bay of Shielings or strange rocks
Cannel	*Cann*yel	
Carsaig	*Car*saig	
Celt	Selt	
Chasgidle	*Ha*sgidil	
Clachaig	*Hlacha*ig	Stony
Cnoc Fhada	Crok-*hada*	Long Ridge
Crakaig	*Craa*kaig	

Place Name	Pronunciation	Meaning
Cruit	*Croo*ht	Celtic Harp (rock similarity)
Dalriada	Dal*riada*	Field or land of Riada (a Celtic prince)
Dervaig	*Der*vaig	The Little Grove
Dhuhearteach	Doo*herta*	Black Death (reef)
Duart	*Doo*art	Dark Headland
Dun da Ghaoithe	Doon da G*eu*	Hill of the Two Winds
	('eu' as in French *feu*)	
Eachann, Lachann	*Eh*ann, L*a*hann	Hector, Lachlan
Eas	Ace	Waterfall or cataract
Eilean	*Ee*lan	Island
Eoghann a 'Chinn Bhic	Ewen a 'Hinn Veek	Ewen of the Little Head
Fionnphort	Feen-fort	White port (sands)
Frisa	*Free*sa	Chill loch
Gillean	Gill*ane*	Name of progenitor Maclean
Glacgugairidh	Glac*hook*ary	Hollow of the Dark Grazings
Gometra	*Go*metra	Island
Gribun	*Gree*bun	
Gruline	*Groo*len	Place of gravel or pebbles
Haunn	*Haa*wn	
Innevea	Inne*vay*	
Kilfinichen	Kilfinihen	'Kil' – cell or chapel of missionary; can also be 'coille'; a wood
Killiechronan	Killie*hro*nan	'Killie' – coille, singing wood
Kintra	Kin*tra*	
Lathaich	La*hay*	
Ledaig	Lay-chack	Local sound – Tobermory
Loch	Lawh	
Lunga	*Loon*ga	Long Island
Maclean	Mac*lane*	Son of Gillean
Mallaig	*Mall*aig	
Mingary	*Min*garry	Smooth grazings
Muracha Gearr	Mooraha *Gya*rr	Short – humpy – powerful Murdoch
Oban	*Oh*ban	Small harbour
Pennyghael	Pennygale	Part of a pennyland, a unit of rental
Reilig Odhrain	*Rayli* Oran	Oran's cemetery (Iona)
Reudle	'eu' as in French *feu*	
'S Airde Ben	'*Sars*te Ben	High hill or promontory

Place Name	Pronunciation	Meaning
Salen	*Sah*len	Salty place
Scarbh	Scarav	Cormorant
Seilisdair	*Shee*lister	Yellow iris
Sguabain	*Skoo*aban	One of the Fingalians
Speinne	*Speen*yih	
Spelve	*Spel*vay	
Sunipol	*Soon*ipol	
Tobermory	Tobber*morry*	Local speech – Well of Mary
Tuath	Tuah	North
Uamh	*Ooa*v	Cave

NOTE   In clan names beginning with 'Mac' the emphasis should *always* be on the main title, not 'mac', which simply means 'son' or 'descendants' of some progenitor; for example. Mac*Lean*, Mac*Donald*, Mac*nab*, Mac*Dougall*, Mac*Neill* and so on.

FURTHER READING

Collier, Alain. *The Crofting Problem* (Cambridge University Press, 1953)

Fraser Darling, F. *West Highland Survey* (Oxford University Press, 1955)
    'Mull is some of the most fertile land in the Kingdom but ruined by sheep farming . . .
    Mull and Ulva are cattle country equal to the best in the Highlands.'

Hill Jacqueline, and O'Grada, Cormack (eds). *The Vengeance of God* (Lilliput, 1994)

Mackenzie, Alexander. *History of the Highland Clearances* (Alex Maclaren & Sons, Glasgow)

Macnab, P. A. *Highways & Byways in Mull & Iona* (Luath Press, 1990)

Macnab, P. A. *Mull & Iona* (David & Charles, 1970)

Proceedings of the Royal Commission (Highlands and Islands) 30 volumes (1892)

Statistical Accounts (1792, 1795, 1845)

INDEX

Page numbers in *italic* indicate illustrations